Table Of Contents

<u>Dedication</u>

First and foremost, God of all creation who graciously gave the ability to make this happen. Without him, none of this is possible.

To my husband, Tweety Angwenyi, we did it baby! You encouraged me to see it through! Thank you.

To our Apostle Calvin Williams, First Lady Shawnee Williams, and the entire Kingdom Advancement International Ministry family, thank you for loving, nurturing, and supporting us.

To my parents, family, and friends, I love you. Thank you for your continuous support.

To my students who have inspired me to *do* more than I say. You are winners, overcomers, and purposeful! I love you all to LIFE.

To every Faith Boss whose eyes and hands have touched this book, you ready? Let's GO!!!

I.Introduction

"For in the gospel the righteousness of God is revealed, both springing from faith and leading to faith [disclosed in a way that awakens more faith]. As it is written and forever remains written, "THE JUST and UPRIGHT SHALL LIVE BY FAITH."- Romans 1:17

You've opened this book because you may identify yourself as a boss, leader, or entrepreneur. You may find ease in taking the lead on projects. You're bursting with new ideas at any given moment. You're a visionary who possesses strategies to improve any organization that you're a part of. You're set apart, called to curate, and a problem solver. You may be all of this and possibly unsure of your assignment in Christ. Rest assured, you're in the right book.

A boss is known as a leader that drives their organization or company in excellence with their ideas, systems, and organization. Most bosses are accustomed to being in full control of their organizations, sitting at the head of the table, and having the highest net worth. They're privy to things being moved around within the company. They're aware of the strengths and weaknesses of their employees. They drive the vision and mission of the company. They have the first say on the culture of the company and the final say on the velocity of it.

They understand marketing, how to gain traction with customers, and get paid to strategize. The average boss, however, is usually missing one vital ingredient in their endeavors that limits their success and overall reach: faith.

This book is not a "how- to" but a "why- to". While reading it, my prayer is that your visions for where God wants you in business will become clearer. Your fear will excuse itself and your faith will reveal things to you. It's important that you know how many people are depending on your obedience in your Faith Boss journey. To be clear, my intentions are not to have you "speed up" your entrepreneurial or leadership journey, but it is my plan to aid you in seeing it through, press beyond moments of doubt and worry, draw out your intentions, and definitely seek God in all things.

Here's to consistent commitment, innovative thoughts, and nonstop insane moments of courage. Here's to your legacy, impact, and God sized visions. There are many who can rightfully claim the role of a "boss", but not many walk in faith while doing it. There are many who are able to make money, delegate to others, and walk in authority, but not many are operating in obedience to their assignment.

By taking the step in reading this book, You may have been introduced to your purpose or still waiting on some confirmations from God. There's a gift stirring up in you that sends your spirit into overdrive and your feelings have no reign over it. There's something inside of you that silences all of the words of doubt and conquers everything that the world asks of you. That's what truly bosses you up: faith.

This journey is for those who are tired of rejecting their gifts, talents, and ideas. This is for those who want to go from the couch to the conference room. This is for the overcomers who are no longer overthinkers. This is for my faith bosses who have managed the shallow end of the pool, but want to go deeper. If you're ready to let go of your own will, break, build, and boss up, you're in the right book.

In this book, you'll find truth, grit, accountability, vulnerability, and encouragement as you embark on your faith boss journey. All of our journeys are different and that's what makes them count. You may identify as an entrepreneur, aspiring entrepreneur, visionary, doer, creative, etc., but the journey of being a Faith Boss requires obedience, patience, and much more than natural capabilities. Many confuse faith with just taking a risk, but it's so much more. Faith is a commitment to trusting God regardless of what you see.

This book is not about guaranteed 7 figure salary or a 300% Instagram follower increase in the next 90 days. This book, unlike others, however, does have some guarantees.

1) You will not be able to deny who your CEO is.

2) Resource after resource that will confirm that God's plan for your life exceeds your own.

3) A confirmation that you CAN do what God has told you to do.

This book is for all of the "No's" that the world gives to you. It's for those who may be able to identify with being stuck or forgotten about. This is for those who are ready to boldly walk into their purpose with no second thoughts. This is for those who don't fear mistakes or barriers. It's for those who are ready for every step whether it's a plateau or a slippery slope.

It's for you. This is about change. This is about leaving fear in hell where it belongs and identifying what's really important: faith.

I. The Right Investment

Of every investment opportunity available in business, faith seems to be the emergency stock. It's one with no risk and high reward. It does, ironically, cost you everything. Our thoughts, apprehensions, plans, and overall structure for how we see our lives pales in comparison to what God has for us. His expectation is that we ditch our own expectations and follow him. This can be a challenge. The Lord knows that we'd struggle with not seeing, but still believing.

"Jesus said to him, " Because you have seen me, do you now believe? Blessed [happy, spiritually secure, and favored by God] are they who did not see and yet believed [in Me]." - John 20:29

Belief alone shapes the way we pursue all things. Belief is the ingredient that transforms an idea into something tangible. Belief, specifically, is not something you see. You either wholeheartedly trust it or don't. The tricky thing about belief is that it can be rooted in *anything* you wish to manifest. Faith, however, is rooted in Christ. We know that without faith, it's impossible to please God. Belief can usually stop short of recognition of something.

Belief precedes the activation of faith. For so long, I thought it was acceptable to only believe in God and never *actually* fine tuned my faith. This led me to believing, moreso, in my own abilities and calling on God when I felt it necessary. We're told from birth that a large part of self-esteem is believing in ourselves. Believing in ourselves is essential to showing up in all areas of our lives. The issue comes about when we apply the same impact of biblical faith to faith in our own works.

To be spiritually poor is to live a life without faith. Faith is our currency. It's how we counteract earthly 'flash sales' of fear, doubt, worry, anxiety, and depression. Jesus paid the price for us to be able to exercise our faith. We didn't earn our redemption because of our talent and wit, we've been gifted redemption because we belong to Christ. There is nothing that we can add to God. He's infinite and sovereign. He, however, loves us so much that as we deny ourselves, he expands our faith to better serve and bring souls to him.

Plenty of people *believe* in their business wholeheartedly, but have no room for faith in allowing God to spearhead their business. The self-made mentality leads us to believe that we're to credit for our success and influence. In our own efforts to make an impact, we may end up making money and gaining traction in our businesses. Our human will can take us places, but will only stray us further from the throne of grace. There are millionaires and billionaires who are struggling with obtaining peace and joy, but have all of the riches that some would argue could buy happiness.

Faith is such an unpopular topic in a world that promotes that we just figure things out on our own. When we're looking to start a new venture, we realize we need seed money or an initial investment. Many people don't mind using the word "faith" to justify their start to building their business. Many have discussed taking a "leap of faith" when leaving their job to start their business, but faith is rarely discussed *after* the initial leap.

Faith is not meant to just be seed money. It's not meant to just get us started; It's meant to keep us going. Faith is seen as a difficult concept if we've only ever placed our belief on what we see. Faith, in fact, may make us look and sound even crazier to someone who builds their intentions on limiting statistics that the world gives. While there are various studies available about why people *shouldn't* believe in God, it's in the word of God that impossibilities actually exist that believers can freely access.

While being a Faith Boss shouldn't be reduced to a calculated risk, our alignment with Jesus has the highest return on investment. In him, we find a source and gain access to resources. In him is our blueprint, our structure, our influence, and overall impact.

Would you believe me when I say that being well-versed about your industry may make you a boss, but not a Faith Boss? Would you argue with me if I said that having leadership skills alone does not make you a Faith Boss? If you're one who has vision and can forecast how the market is going to receive your product or service, that's just a piece of the pie, but still not evidence of faith. Here's a big one: you may be a multimillionaire who has created streams of generational wealth, by working hard, saving money and putting money back. Without God, it's seedless fruit and will not reproduce.

What's missing? Where's God in your business? Whether you own a lemonade stand or a multifaceted corporation, owning a business requires work. Work is not something that bosses tend to avoid, it's submission. The thoughts around submission are that it exposes our weaknesses and makes us feel inferior. We tend to build a tough exterior even in the midst of being overpowered by life's circumstances. When we're calling the shots, we can expect predictability and feel like we're in control of the outcome...until we aren't.

In my own efforts to figure things out on my own, I've come across situations where I've lost control, looked for answers in everything but God, and felt helpless. All of the control that I thought I had ended up reducing me back down to size. I ended up calling back out to the same God that I walked away from when it felt like I had better plans.

In our minds, we may never feel like we're serving another God, but this doesn't stop us from worshipping idols. One of the easiest idols to overlook is ourselves. We live in a world full of self made millionaires and not enough Faith Bosses. The culture of building an empire can easily make us build an altar upon our own name.

Business can be such a finicky game and it's tempting to not say "I made it" when you feel like you actually have. When you look at all of the sweat equity, tears, and sacrifices that you've made to accomplish something, our pride tells us that we should let others know how hard we've worked. To be fair, nothing should discredit hard work, but everything is discredited when we forget who made it all possible.

We tend to think we only need faith when we're in a desperate place. This is why the redemption stories of "taking a leap of faith" are so relatable. Many of us have been in that place where all we could do is depend on God because we felt hopeless. Faith Boss, God is not an emergency button. He's the same God in your redemptive hour as he is in your darkest hour. The truth is we don't strengthen our faith if we only see it as essential in a moment of lack. If we only look to the hills when we're in our valley, how then will we ever grow?

Regardless of where you are in this journey, never forget that God loves us so much that he gave us the gift of repentance. Repentance is the opportunity to make a complete 180° turn from where we are. In faith, we surrender to the will of God for our lives and everything he's purposed us for. The world will convince us that we're meant to go *far* when we're actually meant to go *deep*. YOU are meant to solve problems, serve as a change agent, and do it as a representative of Jesus Christ.

I've been one with many visions and one who has also made many excuses. I've sat on assignments because of fear and made investments that caused me to lose out on what God has for me. I've disqualified myself based on what I thought others would say. I've intentionally tried to be the wallflower. I've been in my shell, I've been in the wrong shell, played small, played too big sometimes, diluted my assignment, and struggled with my identity in Christ.

When asked to speak, I'd find reasons not to. When asked to start something, I'd find ways to pass it to someone else. My resistance to being the one called out made it difficult to realize my purpose. Would I always have reservations about responding to the call? Would God eventually stop calling me to do things? Why was fear crippling me and causing me to shrink?

Out of this, was birthed the #faithboss. I wanted confidence without being confined. I wanted to hear God and trust that if he gave me the vision, he'd share provision. I'd find myself having really vibrant and abstract visions that felt like they had no place in my life. I felt like the visions that God gave me didn't match my own plan. Therefore, I sat on different business ideas and ignored the calling.

My journey of becoming a faith boss doesn't start with a business, plan, or strategy, it starts with obedience. In trusting and listening to God, I've made Christ the CEO of different businesses that he's allowed me to manage. I've been able to deviate from generational curses and expectations. I've been able to do more with the wisdom of Jesus than I have my college degree. Being a faith boss has given me opportunities in industries that I have no background in. Ultimately, it's given me the sensitivity to understand what's *missing* from the entrepreneurial community, **faith**.

There are so many different types of bosses who are dominating the marketplace with goods and services. It feels like there's a community for each of these bosses to spread their wings and support one another. What tends to happen is that Christians who are entrepreneurs don't dominate the amount of space that we should. There's countless creative individuals who follow Christ who are making major moves in film, beauty, technology, education and other industries, but there aren't many discussions of ministry in the marketplace and Christian creatives. Are we being timid with our gifts? Are we afraid to disrupt the industries that don't mind disrupting our belief? More importantly, does faith and business require compromise?

- How are we able to run our businesses and grow in faith?
- How are we able to worship God and serve his people through our creativity?
- Where are the Christian movies that are dominating the mainstream...that aren't cheesy?
- Where is the storefront where we're able to pray with our customers?
- Where is the space where we don't need to compromise and can be free to create, build, and brand our companies?

A #faithboss knows that God has plans for them, trusts him to guide those plans, and willingly represents his creativity and order. You differ from other kinds of entrepreneurs because of obedience to God's plan and not just a plan of making money and influencing others. You're not shaken by the size of a trial or barrier, but encouraged and confident that God will never leave nor forsake them on this journey.

Very early in life, whether we know it or not, we learn to quantify success. We begin to take pride in how much we can obtain in as little time as possible. We begin to want more because we believe having more equates to happiness. Unfortunately, most people substantiate this method of life and will adopt this mentality until the very end of their days.

As a millennial, I've been guilty of falling into the category of one who wants microwaveable success. Unabashedly, I'd say I even felt entitled to have more, do more, travel more, earn more, and essentially be more than anything else I'd seen around me. If it seemed foolproof, you could bet that I'd consider it even if it meant that I'd be willing to go without God. Our generation is conditioned to looking like we have the very best out of the world even if we don't. Ironically enough, it was those very same foolproof plans that gave me no peace. It was those sleepless nights where God put a heavy word on my mind that I tried to fall back to sleep on.

Surely, I couldn't be the only one who has tossed and turned on their assignment and failed to be obedient to the word of God. Like anyone else who's felt this way, I used to feel like God was only worth listening to if he gave me a word of prosperity or any other wealth of promises about what I'd already planned for myself. Yes, it's twisted, but it was the ceiling of my faith.

When we're afraid of the unknown, we begin to cling to the very thing that destroys us slowly: comfortability. Whether it's binge eating to drown our feelings out, mishandling our body for temporary pleasure, submerging ourselves in monetary gifts, or distracting ourselves with what society presents to us. Our comfortability limits our faith and keeps us stagnant.

As a Faith Boss, your reward doesn't look like everyone else's. As people, we can become so programmed to the dimly lit reality around us and never dare to look up. Many have affirmed themselves with mustard seed faith that can move mountains, but what if God is calling you to something larger than mountains? As my Apostle Calvin Williams says, "Just because it's all you need doesn't mean that it's all that you can have."

God is so much to us, but he's also our very first investor. He knows that his word will not return to him void and that #FaithBosses speak life in dark and forgotten places. With full trust in God's plan for us, we're guaranteed exponential growth that won't be understood by the world. As we verse ourselves into more wisdom about business and God, let's never forget that our full investment changes our trajectory and we seek to submit our will to him, bring souls to Christ, and change the narrative for bosses.

"Be on guard; stand firm in your faith [in God, respecting His precepts and keeping your doctrine sound]. Act like [mature] men and be courageous; be strong. Let everything you do be done in love [motivated and inspired by God's love for us]."

1 CORINTHIANS 16:13-14 AMP

II. Called For More

I remember the struggle I had with understanding that I was chosen by God. The struggle was twofold. 1) Why would God choose me? What was his expectation of me? 2) WHO did God not choose?

When being introduced to Christ, we begin to ask about our purpose and calling. We begin to think that Christianity has a *look* instead of a *lifestyle*. Some of us get stuck at <u>Step 1.5</u>: Accepting Jesus Christ as our Lord and Savior and accepting the call of discipleship, but what exactly am *I* called to?

You, my dear, are called for more. You are called for bringing others back to Christ. You are called to love, the greatest commandment. You are called into the transformative light of Jesus Christ. This means you have permission to never be the same because you're forgiven. You are called to overcome things that once easily beset you as Christ has already overcome the world and Christ is in us.

*But you are a chosen people, a royal priesthood, a holy nation, God's special possession, **that you may declare the praises of him who called you out of darkness into his wonderful light.**Once you were not a people,* *but now you are the people of God; once you had not received mercy, but now you have received mercy.- 1 Peter 2:9-10*

This means your calling is not limited to one career or one income bracket. It's not limited to just looking fly on social media and obtaining a level of status. The word *calling* is a pull or urge in a direction. Your calling is not one destination. As children, we were taught to seek one career path and devote the rest of our working days to it. I, somehow, was under the impression that I could make plans for my life that would happen simply because I planned for it.

Faith Boss, by now you know that your plans for your life are vastly different than what God has set out for you. In fact, we don't even KNOW the plans for our life. Sometimes, it's our desire for stability and control that makes us think that our plans are solid and foolproof.

I identified that I was called to entrepreneurship as a teenager. Very early, I felt an urge to create a space that I needed and didn't see. Storytelling was my outlet early on because I loved reading. My assignment has been writing for a long time. The Holy Spirit has guided me to write through trauma, confusion, and joy. It's created a space for me to articulate my needs and take them back to Christ.

As I learned of Christ, I realized that he is the ultimate influencer and wanted to see more faith-based businesses. Even in my own research, I discovered the amount of businesses that I'm a consumer of that were founded on biblical principles, but didn't operate on biblical principles.

As consumers, we invest in the vision of the company. Every transaction is an agreement. Every time we share the news of a sale or new products, we're sharing the gospel. Every time we lead someone to purchase, we're discipling. I mention this because of the sincere need to see FaithBosses at the forefront running businesses in the name of Christ. Christ is the calling. He's our direction.

So I know what may be crossing your mind and I don't fault you for it. What's the difference in being a boss and a Faith Boss? Isn't the entire point to make money, start an empire, build a brand, create a legacy, and did I mention make money? While many will simplify the role of a boss to that of one taking charge, giving orders, and reaping the benefits. A faith boss first submits to God, claims authority over dark and forgotten places, leads others into the light, and embarks on vision. This is the first call.

Whether you're struggling in your faith, business, life, or all of the above, you're in the right book. These words are not meant to inspire you based on what I think. This isn't some janky formula for making millions in 30 days or a scheme to make you invest into someone else's vision while concurrently "being your own boss". This is for those who don't mind putting in a little elbow grease and allowing their faith to land them wherever God assigns them.

All good bosses have a mentor/authority figure/business model that they follow, some are living, some are dead, but none are everlasting. None are self sacrificing and forever forgiving. Most importantly, most mentors or 'bigwigs' at business meetings don't GIVE you vision, they just aid in the facilitation.

Then, here comes our creator loving, leading, energizing, and moving heaven and earth JUST because we have an idea. Here he is again allowing us to truck over barriers and mental lapses just because we write it down and can see it happening. Now, watch as you begin to hear his voice and feel his presence when you BELIEVE that he can and will make this vision tangible.

Allow the CEO to *call* you into the office and continue to call you. Allow the calling to direct your every move. You were chosen for this. It's not by happenstance that you are where you are. Regardless of the trials that are accompanied by it. The calling on *your* life is just a seed for the calling on the lives of future generations. Your obedience serves as a deposit for their reach.

III. The Quitting Disease

Today's trendy entrepreneur has a very predictable formula. Quits/loses job and begins to hustle + takes Instagram photos and lives the very best life on social media - personal downfalls or anything that would hint at failing in an entrepreneurial journey= successful and influential entrepreneur. There's this very shallow expectation followed by general acceptance that entrepreneurs can and should leave a job that was given to them as a means of income because they're unhappy. The larger misconception is that this *chance* that was taken is **faith**.

I can recall each and every moment that I decided that I would quit different jobs in the past. Whether I felt blatantly disrespected by management, failed by teammates, disagreed with the direction of the company, felt overwhelmed from completing other priorities, felt so stressed that it affected my health, or got shorted on a check. All were feelings. All of the feelings felt valid, but I couldn't help but feel like I was abandoning an assignment if I left.

I would admire people who could walk away from things, people, and assignments easily. My fear of quitting was hardly ever rooted from fear of instability (somehow, I knew I would figure it out), but the fear that I was abandoning something. That I, somehow, was walking away from something God called me to...even if for a short season. Now, I'll be the first to say that your kids cannot inherit your job and jobs tend to treat their employees as replaceable items. To be clear, this is not a designation for you to make your job an idol or an enemy..

We have a way of walking away from everything that doesn't serve us. Maybe, just maybe, it's not supposed to serve us. Maybe we're called to serve there. If you're in a position of work politics and it never seems that you can get the right kind of support from your management or teammates, maybe that uncomfortability is supposed to teach you how to lead when it's your turn.

We know that there are seasons in life. There's a season for everything. God is very clear about closing and opening new seasons. There are successful people who have lost jobs, trusted God, and ended up tripling their salary and freeing their family from debt and poverty. There are successful people who have worked as an employee for years, ran a side hustle, and God created a way for them to leave their job. God works in order. Faith without works is dead. We cannot just stop in the middle of the assignment, That's not faith, it's impatience.

Don't be like them, for your Father knows exactly what you need even before you ask him!- Matthew 6:8

The Lord knows exactly what you need in your specific season. Yes, I've dreamt my wildest entrepreneurial thoughts in the midst of working a 9-5 and felt like it couldn't have been more inconvenient. In my time working for someone else, I've grown frustrated with practices, work culture, and everything in between. The frustration, however, wasn't growing me towards Christ. I started losing my savor, half-completing my tasks, and eventually becoming the very thing that I once complained about.

The "quitting disease" is lack of faith. Sometimes you don't ever have to turn in a two weeks notice before quitting an assignment. You, at one point, prayed for where you've complained about. Our missions aren't always glamorous, but they're meant to increase our faith.

Don't mistake me. A circumstance that brings us suffering or struggling doesn't automatically mean that our faith is increased. A common misconception that Christians have gotten a bad rep for is the belief that suffering will bring us closer to God. Correction: suffering without knowing and applying the word of

God is just suffering. This is what the rest of the world does when faced with opposition. When we've been flexing our muscle of faith, suffering may catch us off guard, but will ultimately produce perseverance.

Therefore, since we have been justified through faith, we have peace with God through our Lord Jesus Christ, 2 through whom we have gained access by faith into this grace in which we now stand. And we boast in the hope of the glory of God. 3 Not only so, but we also glory in our sufferings, because we know that suffering produces perseverance; 4 perseverance, character; and character, hope. - Romans 5:1-4

The truth is that ALL humans will struggle and go through trials. The reason that Christians rejoice in being tested is because of the tools that God gives us to endure. This means that while the entire world is trying to climb their mountain, we've boldly told our mountain to move. It's often been misinterpreted that a season of hardship will produce strength, but that's only true if there's faith. Otherwise, it's just hardship.

None of us are exempt from storms. God may have you on a job that you aren't fond of because he's trying to grow something in you. You may feel like there's always a shortage of finances, but he could be teaching you stewardship.

God may have made a way for you to pursue your business full time, but he's teaching you to depend on him in months of overflow *and* months of scarcity.

But my God shall supply all your needs according to his riches in glory by Christ Jesus.- Phillipians 4:19

I'm not encouraging you to sit in a painful position or circumstance. I'm encouraging you to use wisdom and not to put your feelings in authoritative control. There are questions that we can take to God when we're confused. Growing up, it was common to be advised to never question God. God cares more about *where* the question is coming from as opposed to *what* the question is. Our questions should be rooted in faith with no room for doubting. If we're doubting, do we really have a question or is it a complaint?

If any of you lacks wisdom, let him ask God, who gives generously to all without reproach, and it will be given him. But let him ask in faith, with no doubting, for the one who doubts is like a wave of the sea that is driven and tossed by the wind. -James 1:5-6

Now is NOT the time to quit any assignment that you're on. In due time and due season, you will reap. This season may be developing you in faith for the very thing you've been praying for. The vision that God has given you requires a level of faith and endurance that quitting simply won't solve.

IV. Brokivation

Broke + Motivation

Brokivation is a common place where many businesses have been birthed. It's the fight or flight knee-jerk reaction when we're facing lack. In college, I was broke. College broke is a different kind of broke, my friend. My introduction to the practice of entrepreneurship was because of a girl I knew who would text me every morning before class and ask me if I could draw on her eyebrows for $5.

You read that right. $5 and eyebrows. All in the same sentence.

Since this is before the days of CashApp and instant electronic money transfers, I would gladly accept her request, take out my cheap and unknown makeup products, and proceed to bring sis' eyebrows to life.

It taught me something. Okay, it actually taught me a *lot*.

 1) The very thing that you may see as insignificant could be the very thing that people see value in.

2) People pay for convenience. I'm not sure if she knew how to do her makeup or not. It didn't matter, she was paying and I needed money.

3) There's a different kind of work ethic that's birthed out of you when you're broke, facing hard times, and challenged.

4) God has given each of us tools and opportunity. It's up to us to make it work for us.

5) If it makes dollars, it makes cents...and sometimes only cents.

Brokivation is also known as side-hustling. The mentality of never wanting to go without or being broke fuels this hustle. In many instances, many people have started side-hustles that somehow accidentally turned into a full fledged business. This isn't necessarily a bad thing. God wants us to increase and cover more territory, but with him in mind.

When "brokivated", your primary motivation is to never be in lack when it should be to please God. I truly believe that God does not want us to be broke and gives provision in his word about stewardship for that very reason. In this brokivated territory, we can become obsessed with the sales, clients, retention rate, and any way to increase.

The bible is clear that "No one can serve two masters, for either he will hate the one and love the other, or he will be devoted to the one and despise the other. You cannot serve God and money." -Matthew 6:24

God doesn't want us serving from a lack mindset when we've been set free. This isn't to be confused with forgetting where we've come from. There should be a sincere appreciation from where God has delivered all of us from, but we do not have to submerge ourselves back into a place that we once prayed to get out of.

There are people who work to *escape* and people who work to *prepare.* Simply put, there are those who work to never experience poverty or lack again and those who work to set the stage for generations to come. The difference is that one person is constantly comparing themselves to who they've *been* and the other has stored their treasures in heaven while being diligent on earth. If we're constantly working while looking in our rearview mirrors, we'll miss all that God has for us and never actually elevate past our own definition of success.

We'll constantly feel haunted when something reminds us of the past. Could it be that as hard as we've worked to no longer be broke, we've made it an idol and never *actually* got delivered from the poverty mindset? The poverty mindset has hardly anything to do with income. It will constantly tell you that you don't deserve to have better and in so many ways, it will convince you to never *be* better. When we operate from a place of lack, we've counted ourselves out of God's promises for us. The poorest people are those who ONLY have money. There is a difference between *contentment* and *stagnancy*. God calls for us to be *still*, not *steel* (hardened and unchanging).

Instead of chasing the finite riches of this world, we have to learn how to submit to God and go where he tells us. Brokivation might work for a good "come up", but I don't want to run from something my entire life that I know God has already delivered me from.

$5 eyebrows may have introduced me to entrepreneurship and brokivation, but the promises of God remind me that I'm a #faithboss. I'm an overcomer and my works are not only for my own good, but the good of the Kingdom.

Side hustles are a reminder that God gave us talents and skills to generate income. Whether we sharpen them or not is completely on us, but we're to never take them for granted. God may have called you to be a disruptor in an industry and you're over here busy being brokivated. The "doing enough to get by" attitude is not where God called us to be. God speaks in absolutes and won't tell you to half-do something or entertain our satisfactory mindsets.

It's important that if you're one who is moving in the direction of discovery that you motivate (not brokivate) those around you. Encourage yourself as well as those around you to submit those profound ideas to God and even ask for clarity on side-hustles. Sometimes we just make ourselves busy and call it business.

In this #faithboss journey, many distractions will arise. Oftentimes, we can be our biggest distraction. Comparison has been a thief since the days of Adam. Brokivation is temporary motivation and only helps us maintain the shallow end of what God has told us to manage. By picking up this book, I can confidently say that he's calling you deeper. He no longer wants you to operate from brokenness. Allow your brokenness to be a testimony and attest to his transformation of your life. God wants you to consistently call on him to sharpen your tools, not only in the hour of hustle.

V. See-E-O

Thy word is a lamp unto my feet, and a light unto my path.-Psalm 119:105

It's hard to move forward when you don't see where you're going. Many will even be reluctant to make the first step if it's unknown. If we believe that the word is a lamp unto our feet, that means we simply cannot see our journey without God. This is more than simply consulting God, but walking with him.

In creating a brand, we must understand that our operations are constructed by God. He leaves instructions in our hands to complete tasks. He serves as our CEO and we act as the See.E.O. With the vision that's been granted to us, we act as a servant leader who is ***Setting Executive Orders*** while Christ is our Chief Executive Officer.

Like any other organization, there's serious communication flowing from the top down. The vision of the company is in the hands of the CEO. The transformative power for the company also rests in the CEO's hands. The next set of important hands are those that carry out the vision and bring it to life.

At the conception of a brand new idea, there's many questions about the direction. We can almost find ourselves obsessing about the outcome more than the process. I'd argue that many visionaries who see things before they happen, are only privy to a portion of the vision. Being a See.E.O is less about you *seeing* where you're going, but seeing yourself with God wherever you go.

You may be familiar with the verse from *Habakkuk 2:2* ""*And the Lord answered me, and said, Write the vision, and make it plain upon tables, that he may run that readeth it.*"

When we can SEE ourselves somewhere, the word directs us to write it down. There's a different level of accountability in taking something from your mind to writing it down. Once it's written, you can then articulate it if ever approached about it. When someone asks you about your dream, there's more of an ease in delivering the details. This is important.

The "make it plain" aspect of the verse can ironically make things more difficult. So how am I supposed to make this grand, elaborate dream *plain?*

In one particular season of my life, I remember God giving a very specific vision to me. So very specific that it scared me. It was my sophomore year in college and I was home for summer break. During the semester, I'd been on a journey to find peace after a lot of self-inflicted chaos. I was a part of a campus ministry and a brand new "serious" Christian. So I struggled praying, hearing from God, listening to music, and pretty much adjusting to my new life.

God gave me the vision for RelentlessFaith when I was struggling with trying to maintain my own identity. He actually showed me reaching other young women and encouraging others to have kingdom businesses and influences. I literally saw myself THERE, but I couldn't see how my current "then" self could transform into this person that I saw in my vision.

He then reset me. Telling me that my vision wasn't even about me. That I wouldn't even be the face of this movement. He reminded me that faith alone would move mountains, but RELENTLESS faith could move ANYTHING. My choice to be relentless was an attitude shift. This meant not being deterred when told "no", looking past my *then* circumstances, and ultimately being willing to be misunderstood.

For a 20-year old kid in college who had no idea what she was doing, this was next to impossible. Doors kept getting shut, I started feeling less and less normal. The people I used to hang out with didn't see what I saw and our paths were separating. No one around me wanted to fully pursue God because it seemed more like a retirement plan.

In an already dark and confusing place, I started asking God questions about my life. Again, God, the creator of heaven and earth, is NOT threatened by your questions (in faith). I'd placed so much doubt on my life that I couldn't see myself take the first step in faith, let alone accomplish anything else that he planned for me.

I actually started to resent God for revealing it to me because I just wanted to be *normal*. Up until that point, I always felt different. I've never felt my age and just wanted to blend in. I buried myself in shame and counted myself out for God's promises. I felt like I was honestly too much of a mess to be used. Who would listen to me? Who would take me seriously? Again Lord, why me? You've clearly got the wrong address.

I thank God that he saw my purpose more than the pain that I wanted to sit in. I thank God that he used his light to fill every empty space in my heart. When I no longer wanted to be present on earth and convinced myself that no one would care, he plucked me out of the hole of self-pity.

Being a See.E.O is less about seeing yourself and more about seeing God. The steps are ordered and unknown, but the journey is priceless. You are called to set executive order. You may not always see where you're going, but rest assured that you're going somewhere.

One of the first steps to take the first step is accepting Jesus as your Lord and Savior. He's awakened us every morning knowing that there's a possibility that we still may *not* choose him and yet he still breathes life into us.

One thing that I constantly thank God for is choosing me when I didn't have sense enough to choose him. I find it ironic that we'll have questions about walking out our ordered steps with the Lord, but freely walk in whatever direction the world tells us to (especially if others are doing so).

See.E.O, in this season, you've been called to follow his instruction. Your path may look like the odd one out while you're doing it, but your position as a See.E.O gives you oversight beyond the circumstance. You'll be casting the vision, mending the net, and getting your tasks directly from God.

Moses was a See.E.O. Tasked with writing the 10 commandments, he received his directions directly from God in a time where he was uncertain that they would even be received. Joshua, another See.E.O, was given the unusual strategy of instructing his army to march the city of Jericho once a day for six days straight. He organized the soldiers to play their trumpets as the priests carried the Ark of the Covenant. On the seventh day, his army marched around the walls of the city seven times and Joshua assured them, by God's order, that they would see victory.

If you already stick out like a sore thumb, being a See.E.O should be a relatively smooth transition. Most entrepreneurs believe that their hard work should earn them a place of comfortability. Most people wouldn't choose to go to a place where they'll be faced with opposition and *still* lead. Being a See.E.O won't save us from criticism, but it saves us from going the wrong direction.

Our understanding will be tested in this journey as we realize how much we actually don't understand. Our foresight is no longer limited to what others see, but what God has instructed us to do. If you find yourself in an uncomfortable or less than ideal position, posture yourself to hear from God. If he gives you a team or an individual to lead, pray and ask for clarity on where you're leading them. At this time, you were called to see it through.

VI. Vision

"For now [in this time of imperfection] we see in a mirror dimly [a blurred reflection, a riddle, an enigma], but then [when the time of perfection comes we will see reality] face to face. Now I know in part [just in fragments], but then I will know fully, just as I have been fully known [by God]."

1 CORINTHIANS 13:12 AMP

The idea for this book was set into motion over 5 years ago. I received the vision that I would write a book that would help align Christian entrepreneurs back to Christ. The only problem at that time was that I was just beginning my walk with Christ as an adult and felt like I had more questions than answers. I was fearful that pursuing a book about God when I barely had a prayer life was counterproductive. I kept telling myself that I didn't want to lead anyone astray and have to be held accountable for doing so.

In so many ways, I disqualified myself. In my mind, someone with a larger platform needed to write this. God quickly reminded me that a platform does not equate to impact. His favor exceeds numbers, analytics, and subscribers. If he called you to it, he'll bring you through it.

Being a new Christian at that time, I didn't want to come off too "teachy" and "preachy". Not having a full understanding of the trials I was going through at that time, I didn't have the full grasp on vulnerability and full dependence on God. I say all of this to proclaim that God has shown me that it's impossible to ever fulfill anything without him. Many good ideas and much easier assignments have run across my desk, but God mercifully redirected me each time. In this chapter, we'll be discussing *vision*, *provision*, *division*, *envision*, and *revision* as they all relate to God's alignment and plan for you.

Most of us have dealt with some level of insecurity regarding what God has asked us to do. We take a look around and see how others are operating in their assignments and begin to assess our own worth. Doubt kills any dream, but doubt in response to a God-given assignment is rebellion. To have been given a vision accompanied with an assignment and to deliberately NOT do it carries us further away from what God wants for us.

It's possible to glorify fear. Fear usually creates two different types of deception: one where we're afraid to even attempt something because of *fear of failure* and one that leaves us starting things and never finishing it. Ironically, this is called *fear of success*. I sat on this book for years. I sat on business ideas for years. Somehow, I believed God wasn't familiar with my resume. Why would he ask me to do something in an area that I'm weak in? Why would he call me to spark conversations that I didn't have words to contribute to? What happens after I finish what God has asked me to do? What if I fail? Everything seems so much easier if you see someone else do it first. But what happens when God wants YOU to do it first?

The thing that I've learned about vision is that it arrives to us in partiality. This is where faith comes into play. God will give us a vision that may give us insight for a business, project, organization, ministry, but it's not the full picture. 1 Corinthians 13:9 reminds us that *"Now our knowledge is partial and incomplete, and even the gift of prophecy reveals only part of the whole picture!"*

As a #faithboss, asking God about our vision is the first step in accomplishing it. A common mistake that we tend to make is to just see a vision and run with it. God, our CEO, sets the pace of our speed and direction, our velocity. It's in adhering to his counsel that we stop building agendas with incomplete visions. It's understandable why God wouldn't give us an entire vision and leave us to it. Where would the need for him fit in? Oftentimes, when we go without God, our wins end up being our own and our losses end up being his fault.

You may know what it feels like to see something that you're supposed to do and not know where or how we're supposed to accomplish it. Some of us have felt intimidated by our own dreams and felt that they were somehow mistakenly placed in our possession. As my Apostle, Calvin L. Williams, Sr. says, "What you should never forget is the fact that God doesn't call the *qualified* for a position, but qualifies the *called*". Timing, however, is something God is concerned with. Our readiness to submit in obedience and trust God, is an indication of our faith.

Have you ever had an idea for something, doubted it, and within days (or moments) witnessed someone else run off with it? You've probably said to yourself "I literally JUST thought of that."

Now listen.

Did that person run off with your idea or were they just readily obedient?

Ouch.

God gives seed to the sower. Impartation from him requires faith. His will WILL be done and he empowers whosoever is willing. We tend to think that our rank in ministry, education level, or influence usually entitles us to the assignment that God has for us. God isn't moved by how articulate and charming we are. He cares about your willingness, not your wittiness. Our impressiveness works for people, but not for him. Move when God tells you to move.

Isaiah, a prophet, would receive visions. He knew that the Lord was displeased with Judah and the people of God were in rebellion. Isaiah did more with his vision than kept it to himself. He ***envisioned*** bringing people back to Christ. Vision helps us to see what's to come, while envisioning helps us to see ourselves *there*. Spiritually, envisioning should be the ownership we take in our assignment.

"Also I heard the voice of the Lord, saying, Whom shall I send, and who will go for us? Then said I, Here am I; send me." Isaiah 6:8

The world around you may be in rebellion, distraught, in doubt, and ultimately choosing everything but God, but will YOU say yes? Without a doubt, our envisioning should be that of Isaiah's. We should be ready to go regardless of the next step. God has given you a vision and responsibility, now will you be sent? What will you do with your vision?

One thing to note regarding your visions is that in it's premature stage, it doesn't need a lot of opinions. In fact, it may not even need yours. In the book of Genesis, Joseph shares his dream with his brothers and it immediately creates conflict. They met him with questions as they feared that he would one day rule over them.

" Joseph had a dream, and when he told it to his brothers, they hated him all the more. 6 He said to them, "Listen to this dream I had: 7 We were binding sheaves of grain out in the field when suddenly my sheaf rose and stood upright, while your sheaves gathered around mine and bowed down to it."
8 His brothers said to him, "Do you intend to reign over us? Will you actually rule us?" And they hated him all the more because of his dream and what he had said.

9 Then he had another dream, and he told it to his brothers. "Listen," he said, "I had another dream, and this time the sun and moon and eleven stars were bowing down to me."

This doesn't mean that you shouldn't have a community of support while building your assignment, but this is a moment to *reflect*. Just because YOU receive visions on what God has for you, does not mean that other people share that same sentiment. You may find yourself to be the black sheep in different situations due to how you see things. This doesn't mean that anyone in the kingdom of God is any better or worse than the next person, but we all have different functions.

In fact, the lack of support or encouragement in the pursuit of God's assignment for you shouldn't make you fall *away* from people. It should actually make us pray even harder for others. People are ever growing, everchanging, and deserve a chance to learn from their mistakes. Allow disappointment to make you fall closer to Christ.

Joseph even went to his parents and his own family questioned his gift. God knows of the challenges that we'll face when we have to overcome generational curses and limitations. God knows that the weight of it is heavy. Some of you reading this are the first person in your family to break the mold. Some of you may know what it's like to have your intentions questioned and your plans doubted. It's easy to say it's not personal, but it definitely feels that way when it's directed towards you. The enemy likes to take advantage of those feelings and create *division*.

10 When he told his father as well as his brothers, his father rebuked him and said, "What is this dream you had? Will your mother and I and your brothers actually come and bow down to the ground before you?" 11 His brothers were jealous of him, but his father kept the matter in mind. Genesis 37:5-10.

In division, the **vision** has not changed, but it's fragmented and distorted. In division, we're separated from the original intent. Division can come from unresolved conflicts and misunderstandings, lack of knowledge, passivity, distractions, doubt and deviating away from God's will. The longer we nurture division, the further away that vision seems to grasp.

We see this in the pursuit of a dream when we become distracted by anything other than God. It's never our intention to walk away from Christ, but the world is noisy. Division can even occur in a season of prosperity. When everyone is supporting, acknowledging, and praising you for your good works, you then can possibly divide from Christ.

Division and the *partiality* we receive of our vision are two totally different things. When Joseph revealed his vision to his brothers, he only knew of it in part. The vision was actually beyond his understanding because, at that time, it didn't coincide with his present day. Partiality is the intent of God because he wants to grow our faith. His vision for us will consistently unveil as we trust him. Partiality is the reminder that we REALLY don't have to know everything.

The beautiful thing about the story of Joseph is that his purpose never changed regardless of the lengths made to stop it. Shortly after revealing his vision, his brothers plotted to kill him because they were intimidated by his dreams and faked his death after selling him. Even in being sold, Joseph was in charge of all of Egypt. Joseph later confronted his brothers in Genesis 45:4-7 and said

*"I am your brother Joseph, the one you sold into Egypt! **5** And now, do not be distressed and do not be angry with yourselves for selling me here, because it was to save lives that God sent me ahead of you. **6** For two years now there has been famine in the land, and for the next five years there will be no plowing and reaping. **7** But God sent me ahead of you to preserve for you a remnant on earth and to save your lives by a great deliverance."*

FaithBosses, in the very rejection you could possibly face for having vision, your assignment could very well be to uplift those who have despised you. One of the biggest misconceptions that we can have when it comes to dreams is to believe that it's just for **us**. Another misconception is that we get to pick and choose WHO and WHAT our assignments are. It'd be so easy to be assigned to someone or something that didn't challenge us, but God is invested in our growth, not our comfort.

Surely, if Joseph would've bowed to his feelings of betrayal he would've sat on his dream, never spoke up, and even rebelled when placed in a position of power, he would've never fulfilled God's mission for him. FaithBosses, the prayers we have of *elevation* require ***transformation***. The thoughts we have of abundance come with sacrifice. The growth we're wanting to have in our businesses require management of what we currently have. The theme of Joseph's story reminds me of one thing we tend to lose in the daily grind of life: *alignment*.

We know that when things are out of alignment in our lives when things are leaning more to one side than another. Between being obedient to what God has been telling us and hearing the noise from the world, our path can get rerouted.

In a place of being misaligned, God begins to give us ***revision***. This is a result of his mercy and allowing us to work out what we once didn't know how to. In our revision, we must realign with God and truly seek his vision. This time he may ask you to do something different that will require less of you and more of him. In God's revising, he's adding to the plan and rewriting some things for your original vision. The plan never changed, but there's now new instruction.

It's important that as we remain aligned with him, we learn how to make ***provision***. This is God's endless supply of wisdom and word. Provision is his grace abounding and leading us further from excuses and closer to his promises.

Provision keeps us rooted and accountable for the changes that we're in progress of making. In vision, provision acts as the anchor that keeps us grounded in completing what's ahead of us.

Provision is the reminder that God never gives you a vision that you don't need him for. He's provided much for us already and will continue to provide when we ask and submit to him. In the breaking down of the word *pro*-vision, it reminds me that God has the oversight of our vision. That, what we can't see, he sees clearly and sees the generational impact. Circumstances in life, business, family, and every other area can discourage and derail us from the vision that God has given, but that vision never changes. When it feels blurry and uncertain, refer back to the provision.

When struggling in belief, look for his provision. When struggling in fear, look for his provision. When you're overwhelmed, confused, and struggling with finding resources, look for his provision. You should surround yourself with more provisions than doubt. You should share more provisions than business advice. In him, you have everything you need.

His divine power has given us everything we need for a godly life through our knowledge of him who called us by his own glory and goodness.- 2 Peter 1:3

Visionary, while you may feel overwhelmed, misunderstood, or occasionally overlooked, your foresight is going to change things for people. In whatever area of vision that you're in, know that your *envisioning* isn't in vain. Know that *division* doesn't change vision, but it does slow it down and can make it harder to attain. *Revision* means that there's more work to do and *provision* sharpens the vision.

As God gives you vision, be sure to write it down and make it **plain**. In the following table, you'll write down the very specific *visions* that God has given you.

- You'll specify how the vision has developed as you've been *envisioning* it.

- You'll note any moments of *division* and be specific in the root of the division and your plan of resolving it.

- Has God brought you back to the drawing board in *revision*?

- You'll also record all of your *provisions* concerning God's vision for you.

- This list can be continuous and relative to when you receive different visions. You'll add to it as you go along.

Name the vision.	How have you been envisioning it?	Areas of division.	Revision.	List your provisions.
This is a huge part of making the vision plain.	Describe EXACTLY how you see the vision. Be as colorful and detailed as possible.	Where has the vision veered off? If anything, what has come between you and the vision? How do you plan on resolving it using the word of God? Be specific.	What areas are needing changes and additions? What can be worked on in this area to fine-tune the outcome of the vision?	God has already provided all that you need.Go to the word of God and list scriptures that will hold you accountable to your vision.

VII. The Cost of Perfection

"For most certainly I tell you, whoever may tell this mountain, 'Be taken up and cast into the sea,' and doesn't doubt in his heart, but believes that what he says is happening; he shall have whatever he says. Therefore I tell you, all things whatever you pray and ask for, believe that you have received them, and you shall have them." -Mark 11:23-24

Let's imagine that today is *the day*. All systems are rolling, we're approaching the mountain and geared up to climb, but we notice there's a creek hidden along our trek. We take a look at our supplies and realize that the ONE thing that we didn't prepare was something to get across the creek. We simply didn't anticipate needing to swim. Everything that we worked for feels defeated and we come to a screeching halt.

Now we're reconsidering our mission to climb our mountain and seize what's on top. At this point, we want to go home and collect materials to cross our creek. We begin moving into *analysis paralysis* and begin wondering if this mountain was even our assignment.

So maybe you're not going hiking any time soon, but I'm sure you're in the midst of some kind of metaphorical climb. Some days you may feel like you're made for the journey and other days you may question why you're doing it. Both days you need faith.

Due to things not going to *our plan,* we opt out of the race. Faith Bosses, it's ironically in times of pure uncertainty, that our faith needs to be on high. Our faith need not subside due to the mountains that come about. Our human instinct immediately fears failure and plays it safe to avoid it altogether. You will not be able to both play it safe AND operate in the full potential of your assignment. You must choose one.

The book of Proverbs states that *All hard work brings a profit, but mere talk leads only to poverty.* When we have a new idea, we love to talk about it and forecast the plan. The enemy knows that your pursuit in what God has for you will derail his plan for your downfall. Faith stabilizes us and prevents us from wavering in the plan. Faith says "I know" instead of "I think". Faith is beyond our sight. It's not faith when we can see how well things are going. It's faith when things are actually opposite of how you planned them, but you still believe that God's promises will be fulfilled.

The planning phase is a place of opportunity and pure creative vision. The planning phase is also a place where our obedience is tested. Many of us are great starters, but struggle finishing. In my experience, I actually have started many businesses in my mind. Some even made it to paper. Yes, some were really good ideas and some were just fluff and I knew that. God has been very intentional, however, with the things he's wanted me to do. Somehow, in just starting, I thought I was pleasing God.

You read that correctly. Simply by **starting,** I believed that God was pleased and I fulfilled my assignment. The word of God is clear in Philippians 1:6, *"That Being confident of this very thing, that he which hath begun a good work in you will perform it until the day of Jesus Christ."* If God has given you seed, he expects us to water while he manages the progress. Our obedience is tied to the entire process that God has for us, not just the first step.

Trust God in your process of being a Faith Boss. The idea of perfection is a deception given to us that eliminates the need for faith. We know in life that nothing is perfect, but this still doesn't stop us from wanting the best version of something. This issue that comes about is that we rarely consult God in what the actual best version of our project is. We begin to create our own filter for a vision that was his to begin with.

If you find yourself in the midst of trying to win a war of perfectionism, stop fighting. If he started it in you, he'll be sure to see that you complete it. If you take nothing else from this chapter, it's finishing.

Some practical steps to ensure that you finish what you started. Remember, they only work if you do.

1. **Break your big goal into smaller goals**. Our ambitions can lead us wanting to climb an entire mountain in a day. We'll get so amped up on this huge goal that we tire ourselves out before ever taking the first step. Start with small manageable goals everyday that will get you closer to the mountain.

2. **Make time for RESToration**. Psalm 51:12 says "Restore to me the joy of your salvation and grant me a willing spirit, to sustain me." There's a difference between simply laying down and laying down your burdens at the feet of God. We have no problem resting, but we have to learn to take part in restoration. Renewing our mind daily with Christ helps us stay aligned in all things you're involved in.

3. **Count it all joy**. Challenges will come. Mistakes will be made. You'll learn on the fly. You'll fall privately and occasionally stumble publicly, but at the end of the day, it's all joy. James 1:2-4

states "My brethren, count it all joy when you fall into various trials, **3** knowing that the testing of your faith produces [a]patience. **4** But let patience have *its* perfect work, that you may be [b]perfect and complete, lacking nothing."

4. **Set the tone.** There's a lot of noise in the world. There's a lot of criticism that comes forth in an effort to try new things. There's not a lot of people starting things with the intent and purpose of finishing them, ***but you are***. You set the tone by creating an atmosphere for God to flow through. Before going into the workplace, <u>play worship music</u>. <u>Write down scriptures</u> that remind you to finish and ***sit in it***. When your mind starts to wander in doubt or you're not feeling supported, remember that you have the authority to shift any atmosphere with the word of God.

5. **Finish**. Set a deadline. A deadline is for a completed work, not a perfect work. Don't let projects pile up. Erase some of the tabs on your computer. Today, finish one thing. Your finished work may be the first draft or the final draft, but nothing beats finishing it. It's when we finish one thing that our eyes open and we see everything else that we can finish. 2 Corinthians 8:11 reminds us to start things

with the intention to finish. "But now finish doing it also, so that just as there was the readiness to desire it, so there may be also the completion of it by your ability."

Don't allow perfection to rob you of your time. The Holy Spirit drops revelation and assignments on whomever it wishes to in a particular season. God loves the care we take of ideas that he gives us, but he doesn't want us to stall. Time is more expensive than money. We can always make more money, but can never recoup time. Our excuses, doubts, and feelings of insecurity are robbing us of the most expensive asset we have access to. Spend it well.

VIII. Due vs. Do Season

We know that all things happen in an appointed time. There's a time to reap and a time to sow. A time to plant and a time to harvest. There's a time to **do** and time to pay what's **due.** Great ideas come and great ideas go. Profitable ideas come and if we're not careful, they can quickly transform from an idea to an idol.

Today, we're all trying to "do" something to seek something more. Many of our goals are concentrated around obtaining the next level of something. Our "doing" is usually inspired by what WE believe it's right. In "doing" anything, we usually dictate the pace at which it should be done. For example, if I don't feel like running 2 miles today, it simply won't get done until I feel like it. Afterall, it's just something that I "do".

In my job as a teacher, however, there are various "due" dates that I'm given in order to complete my tasks. I give these due dates my undivided effort and priority and there's not much compromise on whether it's going to get done or not. It's interesting to see how we prioritize things daily. When something's due, the pressure of feeling like I owe someone is heavy. It's almost like the fear of losing my job or disappointing someone that trusted me to do something is what pushes me to complete it.

In the journey of entrepreneurship, God gives us "due" seasons and we tend to have "do" seasons. When we're always in motion, we feel like we're chasing success. For so many, success (in whatever way you define it) is what's due. It's the objective, the motive, and what we reach for daily. In doing, we can easily miss what's due.

There are many things we *do* out of routine with no real understanding of what's *due*. Going to church every week and attending every bible study is something that we *do*. In our time alone, our personal praise and worship, our prayer time, how we *treat* others, how we *think* of others, how we *pray* for others, and how we acknowledge God in our lives is what's due...with urgency.

The same heaviness we feel when it comes to our livelihood should be how we see the deadlines that God has given us. He gives us new grace and mercies everyday, but this doesn't take away from what's due. We're here on assignment. Our mission here on Earth isn't even just for us. There are people attached to our obedience and our "Yes". Oftentimes, we're the distraction. We begin doing and never once asking God if it's what's due.

Pride will make us want to scale God's assignments. We may mistake and question the simplicity of what he's asked us to do and build our own extravagant venture. God doesn't need your idea of "better", he needs obedience. Some of us are sitting on late assignments that we're twiddling our fingers to turn in because it's not what we would've picked for ourselves.

He doesn't need us to do it when *we're* ready because it's time sensitive. When a woman finds out that she's pregnant, one of the most important pieces of information that she's given is her ***due date***. From that moment forward, she's growing every day preparing for her due date. Whether the actual date fluctuates or not due to the pregnancy, one thing is for sure...the baby is coming.

We need to see our assignment as a sure thing. When God has asked you to stand in the gap and obediently fulfill what he's asked you to do, regardless of your doing, his will SHALL be done. The due date still stands.

God, the author of time, understands the relevance of setting deadlines. Rest assured, he will not give you a task that you *don't* need him for. This book, for instance, was God's very specific assignment for me at an appointed time.

At the time of receiving the revelation, I instantly rejected it. God, being so merciful, never lifted the assignment from me. He knew that in *due* time, I'd submit and finish what he had for me whether I knew it or not. I created many excuses and segways into not doing it and busied myself with other things.

This chapter serves as a reminder to do what's due. You may have an area in your life where you're simply going through the motions of life and don't have much clarity on where you're going or why you're going. While Jesus was on earth, he knew he had a clear assignment. An assignment that would end in a brutal and undeserved death, but it was *due*. He wasted no time in simply doing because our souls were on the line. He took our lives so seriously that he gave his own. From this moment forward, let there be no late assignments. Let's turn it in on time.

"And in this matter I give my judgment: this benefits you, who a year ago started not only to do this work but also to desire to do it. So now finish doing it as well, so that your readiness in desiring it may be matched by your completing it out of what you have. For if the readiness is there, it is acceptable according to what a person has, not according to what he does not have." -2 Corinthians 8:10-12

IX. Thoughtful Interruptions

I remember when I could stay in bed all day with no desire to see sunshine. I'd avoid calls, cancel plans, and occasionally even call in from work. I just didn't *feel* right. I didn't *feel* like being productive. I just *felt* stuck. Sure, depression would be the fastest diagnosis, but I created a habit out of failure and that was worse. Let me explain.

The faster that we accept that failure is a choice, the more likely we are to stop choosing it. But Patrice, who would be crazy enough to CHOOSE failure? If you can choose to win, you can also choose failure. We usually take in information and filter it through our fear. When approached with a new idea, we measure this idea up to what we know about our capabilities.

It's no secret the enemy's battlefield is the mind. The minute that he can convince us of who we are and what we're not, he's trapped us in our own mind. The only thing that interrupts darkness is light. The very same people who *interrupt* those thoughts with provisions of truth create winning habits.

Let's put it like this, the enemy knows us. He knows our mother, her mother, and our grandmother's great grandmother. He knows what we're predisposed to and what cycles we're fighting to get out of. He knows our insecurities and the things we're trying to overcome. He's aware of our hot buttons and the things that trigger us. The devil will plant a seed and somehow convince us to water it.

I used to wonder why the fight of depression was so heavy on me. I'd be up one minute laughing and joking with others and plummet into darkness within the next few seconds. What was especially confusing was that it was hardly ever circumstantial. It felt so random and unfitting. It felt like anytime I'd try to overcome it with what normally makes me happy, it was temporary. It felt like I was trying to find the joy of the Lord in everything BUT God.

The thing about depression is that it will put you in a routine and no matter how productive you can get, you'll still be unfulfilled. I'd go to work and class everyday. I'd show up for things that I committed to and try my best to be present. I'd oftentimes be surrounded by people and somehow feel like I was the only person in the room. Needless to say, I'd have days I'd function well and other days I wouldn't.

One day, I finally got strategic about the heaviness I was walking in. I realized that there was a place that I could go and not feel attacked, alone, or fearful and it was worship. It was a safe place of pure vulnerability and surrenderance. I was reminded that when I'm standing in the light of God, darkness cannot interrupt it.

When doing business, it's easy to neglect our spiritual maintenance. We somehow learn to numb ourselves from the interruptions and eventually get the job done. While this may seem functional, we're so much more effective when we spend time in the presence of God. God wants us to be physically, mentally, and spiritually well. He wants time and worship from us. He sets provisions before us so that those thoughts get interrupted with the truth.

Find it not strange that the enemy is using his tactics to stop you. He knows what's inside of you and wants to kill it before it grows legs. The enemy is in the business of spiritual abortions and he camps out in our habits. He knows the power of the things we watch, listen to, and even eat. He knows our tendencies and what areas of our life aren't submitted to God. Those are the areas he terrorizes and plots to take ownership of.

12 Dear friends, do not be surprised at the fiery ordeal that has come on you to test you, as though something strange were happening to you. 13But rejoice inasmuch as you participate in the sufferings of Christ, so that you may be overjoyed when his glory is revealed. 1 Peter 4:12-13

Wherever you are in your Faith Boss journey, shame *off* of you. We are not the mistakes of our parents or their parents. We are not inherently doomed by generational curses. We're not slaves to cycles. Many of us grow with shackles on our ideas because of doubt and fear. We grow to never take our own ideas seriously. We begin a vicious cycle that thirsts for validation. Interrupt those thoughts with the truth of God's word. Many people park their assignments and goals for years because of a simple thought that manifested into stagnancy.

In us, God has implanted a purpose, provision, and a will. Neither one requires being understood in every aspect by others. God's purpose isn't contingent upon us being popular, it's contingent on us being obedient.

X. Obedience

In the good book, (not this one, but one much better) nothing is subtle about obedience. Living in a world where nobody answers to anybody, obedience gets drowned out in the hymns of independence. That's right, the VERY word that little girls like myself got taught very early. We're taught to take care of ourselves, not ask anyone for anything, and trust no one. We're essentially taught to take the longest route possible in accomplishing a goal if it means that we did it by ourselves. I hate to be the one to remind you, but there are absolutely positively NO awards for that.

As a young woman of color, you can bet your last coin that I was conditioned to believe that dependency equates to frailty and weak-mindedness. The word 'vulnerable' used to make me gag. The topic of submission would be followed by my footsteps heading to the closest exit. I'll admit it, I hung my hat on being an unbreakable,impenetrable, rock-solid, incredibly smart black woman who could have it ALL. Or at least this is the dream I bought from the world.

I'd be lying to you if I told you that I've been the most obedient person throughout my walk. My "Yes" to God has often been a reluctant one. The real struggle with obedience for me was the fear of having my wings clipped. I've always been taught to think for myself and to never just agree to something without asking questions. It felt like where I was going spiritually just didn't agree with everything that I *thought* I knew. This is exactly where God wanted me.

The struggle was so real for me that I once cried over a birthday cake. Not my own, but a cake I was making for my husband. Now listen, I'm a pretty good cook. Baking, however, isn't necessarily my forte. I wasn't really *taught* how to bake and I occasionally burn premade cookies. Don't judge. I hate admitting that because it means that I have a weakness and other people knowing that I, Patrice D. Angwenyi, have a weakness is a NO to the NO. I could've easily recruited help, watched a YouTube video, or just simply bought a cake, but I was determined to finish what I started and press past my fear of failing.

Usually, when I'm bad at something, I just avoid it altogether. Not just in the simple realm of baking, but in a lot of other areas. I may see it as ONLY watering what I'm good at, God may see it as rebellion. The cancer that I've fed in this area is called *pride* and it keeps us from being obedient and submitting to God. It stunts our growth, slows us down, and limits our reach. The truth about obedience is that it saves you a lot of heartache in the end. Bumping our heads into brick walls is not something that God is fond of seeing us do.

In fact, even delaying what God has told you to do is considered disobedience. Timing is a major part of the recipe. Oftentimes, we delay our obedience because we have questions that are rooted from doubt. God, the creator of the universe and the author and finisher of your faith, is NOT bothered by your questions. Asking questions in faith is something that I believe God wants us to do. I'd even say that oftentimes, we're afraid to ask God certain questions because we don't want the answer. We know it will require a different level of obedience. He wants us to explore him in depth and graduate from our surface level faith.

*Therefore let us move beyond the elementary teachings about Christ and be taken forward to maturity, not laying again the foundation of repentance from acts that lead to death, and of faith in God, **2** instructions about cleansing rites, the laying on of hands, the resurrection of the dead, and eternal judgment. Hebrews 6:1-2*

As FaithBosses, God expects us to advance past the "elementary" things in our walk. After so long, struggling to have faith becomes disobedience. Much like a child that's growing and developing, there's an expectation that they'll graduate from different levels of the process, not entertain the stagnancy for the sake of their comfort. Obedience is celebrating progress, but yet listening to what God needs from us next. Obedience is simply the surrenderence of your own ideas, feelings, and desires and doing what God says anyway.

If you're like me at all, the fear of looking weak, vulnerable, or needy has led me to stagnancy. It felt like God was breaking something in me that I just wanted to keep feeding. I'd find myself saying that I needed *more* of him and he'd let me know that he needed *less* of me. Pride is the impulse to say "I got this" when you really don't. It's the 'self-made', independent, "I don't need help" mindset that leaves people alone, broken, and further away from where they need to be.

It's not odd to see people at the top who deal with pride and are fulfilled with their own accomplishments, but are limited on their impact. There's more of an obsession in looking successful than *being* successful. There's a casualty that we tend to have where we put more effort into our *presentation* than our *posture*. There were times that I'd disobey by knowing I was supposed to pray for others, but I hadn't spent any time with God that week so I didn't want to disappoint anyone. There were times I was supposed to give, but I didn't think what I was giving was enough so I held on to it until it was something I'd be impressed with. Friend, God did not put you on this earth to impress him by your own might. He put you on this earth to please him by carrying out his word. It's very hard to impress a God that created everything. Just saying.

We occasionally forget about obedience when opportunity is present. Want to know what's frustrating? God will have you going through a pruning season where he wants you to be still. If you're impatient and accustomed to making things happen on your own, being still isn't a fun place to be.

Let's clarify that there's a difference between being ***still*** and ***isolating yourself***. Sometimes, when we're accustomed to being in control and everything is moving beyond our control, we retreat to isolation. The world feeds us the lie that isolation protects us from harm. The enemy understands that his job is to bring mischief and make you feel like a failure. He'll remind you of all of the brick walls that you've hit and convince you that it's your fault.

Cheat code: plots from the enemy always result in shame. We'll lose that job, car, house, relationship, etc. and want to hide or defend ourselves from criticism. That business idea that we so badly wanted to flesh out will lose the zest it once had and we'll feel defeated. We result in warring in our mind about if we're good enough. The enemy's intentions are to keep you in this place long enough so that you'll begin to resent God.

I immediately begin to think of Job when I think of obedience and remaining still. Job was literally pushed in the wilderness into a hopeless and nearly impossible situation but was expected to remain faithful. Regardless of anything said to him, his commitment was to please God even if it meant he would die doing so. His faith was unwavering and couldn't be challenged by even those closest to him. Job was a real one. He was willing to follow God if it meant risking it ALL.

God may call you to a place of pure discomfort or a saturated market, but he wants your "yes" without doubt much like Job. The enemy often wants to convince us that the lane that we want to ride in is already occupied. His sole purpose is to distract you with thoughts of doubt and validate it with confusion and insecurity. There are many similar businesses out there, but does this mean that you don't deserve a seat at the table?

When you go into an urban community, there are many fried chicken restaurants. When you drive down a highway, there are many different gas stations. There's various grocery stores on one street. In fact, many of them even have the same owner, but are marketed as different stores. There's multiple nail and hair salons on one street. If one store doesn't have what you want, you simply go to another one, right? Variety builds consumerism. People like options and innovation. Your God-given vision, once submitted, will nurture your gift which will definitely make room for you.

Go where God has told you to go even if your naked eye sees opposition. God's plans exceed ours. Some of you will be called to territories that are unpopular and seemingly unsound. Will you go anyway? Will you follow the instructions of the Lord even if they contradict your own ideas. Will you trust the will and plans he has for your life even if they oppose your own?

The obedience journey is a daily surrender. Every day we trust God and know that he hasn't left us yet and he won't start today.

For I know the plans I have for you," declares the LORD, "plans to prosper you and not to harm you, plans to give you hope and a future.- Jeremiah 29:11

XI. Unbothered

In this chaotic, violent, crazy world, there are actually quite a few reasons to be bothered. If it's not normalizing dysfunction and broadcasting it to the masses or idolizing humans and worshipping material things, one can easily get lost in the sauce of gaining acceptance, being loved, and feeling accomplished.

The truth is that our very fragile shells are usually affected by things happening around us. The true power is in the response. In fact, when we begin to view responsibility as "response-ability", we end up walking in the true light of unbotheredness. Everything doesn't deserve a response and if you can't give your best response, maybe you should pray instead. Well, actually, pray regardless.

But, does Christ call for us to simply 'not care'? Is being "unbothered" anywhere close to where he wants us to be? Should there be a clear line between personal and business matters? The consistent mood of a faith boss is indeed to be unbothered. It doesn't mean that we aren't impacted by others, but our actions aren't contingent upon anything else other than the purpose that God has created.

My first year of teaching was hard. When I say hard, I mean flirting with unemployment was a daily occurrence. Ever felt like God put you in a place that you didn't ask to be in and due to the circumstances of that place, your dependence on his word changed? You went from occasionally indulging in the word of God to falling at his feet before making any decisions. I find that God likes for us to be here. However, in this particular season, I was the furthest thing from unbothered.

I taught 12th grade when I was just 24 years old. Just a year prior, I would tell people how important it was for me to reach back to forgotten communities and empower youth. To combat the disapproving looks on their faces, I would remind them how these kids needed encouragement, an advocate, and most importantly the love of God. Fast forward a year later, I'm standing in a classroom looking at 17/18 year olds who need love and reassurance, but ask for it in the validation of explosive behaviors.

Everyday got easier, but every day was tough. Between the cries out for help and personal attacks, I learned how to stay on post. Sometimes doing *good* doesn't necessarily feel *good*. God didn't intend for us to be soft and NOBODY can check your walk in Christ faster than a child. Believe me.

When we're attacked, it's easy to be on defense but that's not the armor that God wants us wearing. Christ calls us to be on the offense with the word and be intentional in all of our pursuits.

"Listen carefully: I am sending you out like sheep among wolves; so be wise as serpents, and innocent as doves [have no self-serving agenda]."
MATTHEW 10:16 AMP

I find that sometimes it's best to unlearn everything that we think is right and follow our spirit. This, however, isn't easy when all we know is literally ALL we know. It's easy to get trapped in our thoughts when it's always been our shelter. It's easy to respond to someone's criticism with anger if it's all we've ever known. When all we've known is protecting ourselves and defending our own name, the word of God challenges us to defend his name like we try to defend our own.

Much of my struggle in my 'unbotheredness' has been in the bondage of my own thoughts. It's kept me from forgiving, starting and finishing assignments, and in an impenetrable self-protective shell that kept me from opening up and sharing my testimony. The enemy kept me shameful for a long time about what God has brought me from.

Years ago, I was in a depressive and self loathing state. I created an idol out of my own independence and sought to be in situations that I could control. Then I broke. The numbed state that I practiced for so long shattered and revealed who I really was. A broken young woman who cared about ***almost*** everything. I cared about what people thought of me. I cared about who liked me and who didn't. I rarely ever asked God if anything that I was doing or not doing was acceptable to him.

At that time, walking with Christ seemed like I'd be giving up too much. I'd been playing "unbothered" and "untouchable" for so long, it seemed like I was playing my own god. This book was birthed from one of the most broken places I'd been. The minute that version of Patrice died, God's will for my life was born and the journey began.

Being unbothered shouldn't be confused with being careless. Unobothered is a reminder that you shall not be shaken with what comes your way because God has already gone before you.

"Those who respect the Lord will live and be satisfied, unbothered by trouble." - Proverbs 19:23

Things will never stop happening around us. We'll always be challenged as God always wants us to grow. The unbothered FaithBoss seeks to continually sharpen their iron and prepare for what's ahead. This means not getting distracted by trivial matters or allowing circumstances to detour you from your goal.

So, what happens when we're just not THERE yet? What if you're embarking on this unbothered journey and you're actually extremely bothered? Here are some practical steps to being and remaining biblically unbothered:

1. **Respond to what you can control**: Remember when we talked about **response-ability**? When we fully embrace the unbothered lifestyle, we understand that our reactions can intensify things and take us further from a resolution.

2. **Forgive.** Unforgiveness will have us out here *extremely* bothered. The deceptive thing about unforgiveness is that if it's not pulled from the root, it will sprout on to everything else we do.

3. **Focus on things that are high, not low.** Phillipians 4:8 says *"Finally, brothers and sisters, whatever is true, whatever is noble, whatever is right, whatever is pure, whatever is lovely, whatever is admirable--if anything is excellent or praiseworthy--think about such things."* There's always something worthy of thinking and

meditation on. As chaotic as the world around us is, there's still good things happening. There are plenty of things within your life to be obsessively grateful about. While I'm not telling you to disregard things that are unfortunate, this is just a reminder (not a dismissal) that there's always something to thank God for.

4. **Overcoming is always an option**. 1 John 5:4 says *"For everyone born of God overcomes the world. This is the victory that has overcome the world, even our faith."* In your dreariest of days, he will give you a way of escape. Jesus redeemed us in his voluntary sacrifice so that we shall always be reminded that his blood covers us in his acceptance of him. Regardless of what the world will tell us, we always have the opportunity to overcome.

XII. Unwrap This

I'll never forget driving to work one morning and my vehicle spinning out of control into oncoming traffic. I just remember screaming, subconsciously holding my breath, existing in a silent vacuum, and then quickly closing my eyes almost as if to accept what was coming next. When I opened them, I was on the shoulder of the freeway with a truck blowing their horn at me. I exhaled.

Not sure what the psychologist next door would call this, but there's a very distinct taste that gets on your tongue when you're in survival mode and you're in a fight of your life. I was just happy to experience that taste.

Attempting to turn my locked steering wheel, I said in a whisper "Thank you Lord." I still didn't quite believe that any of this happened, but it was rather clear that no one but Jesus Christ was to credit.

Like many others who've cheated death, it was then that I gained perspective on being present and the work that it takes. Amidst all of the laps that our brain does in a day, relicking in the moment has become a full on sport. Who is your competitor? You. What do you get for losing? Lost time, lost opportunity, and manifested fears. The winner, however, gets to take home the incomparable prize of peace.

The best gift we've received is the present. No pun intended. However, it's what we do with the present that makes it rewarding. This book idea came to me in 2014. I wrote and wrote and erased and erased. I either focused too much on the future that had it's on set of worries or the past that has already taken care of itself.

In fearing the future, I wondered if people would read it. What if no one understands what I'm talking about? Do I have anything worthwhile to say? I basked in shame of the past. "I can't share that.", "I remember that, but it's too painful.", "I feel too egotistical about that." I was present in all of the wrong things. All of the fearful things that rob our futures. That's exactly what our doubts do, rob us of the present.

Here's the thing about all of these doubts in response to what God told me to do. It was never about me. Mind blown. I was sitting here assessing time, wasting it while thinking I had an abundance of it, and not ONCE asking the creator of time what to do with it! When we fail to be present, we trade God's grace for our own will. We busy ourselves with our own agendas and fill our time with what makes sense to us.

The 21st century "busy person" usually makes a task out of creating tasks for the future. This is why so many people take part in planning, not that it's bad at all, but when we lose our flexibility and turn a deaf ear to Christ, we become frustrated and complacent. We, ironically, lose more time in trying to make time when we don't prioritize what God wants us to do.

When first learning of Christ, I would be blown away at hearing others discuss the time spent in their prayer closets. Some would talk about how they would be in worship for *hours*. Sis, HOURS??!

In my very calculated mind, I would hit God with a "God is good, good is great" prayer and go on about my day. I would say to myself, "It really doesn't take ALL of that." The more that I dismissed time with God, the more time got away from me. I'd overlook a moment of stillness and call it boring. Moments of chaos called for prayer, but I would just lean into it and respond with what I knew.

After a while, I completely understood why people were spending unrecorded amounts of time at the feet of God. It became less of a chore and more of an opportunity. Mind renewal keeps us present and aligned with God.

This essentially helps us separate the fat from the meat when it comes to our thoughts.

Mind renewal is required DAILY. Dying to our flesh is a daily task. *Okay sis, you said dying and mind renewal all in the same breath, I'm lost.*

2 Do not conform to the pattern of this world, but be transformed by the renewing of your mind. Then you will be able to test and approve what God's will is—his good, pleasing and perfect will. -Romans 12:2

Stay present, FaithBoss. There's a lot of noise and cloudiness in this world. There's many distractions. You, however, can't afford to stop your progress in this walk. You can't afford to walk away from all that you've overcome. Checking out of the present deceives us from what the present offers. Instead of planning for the future and overthinking the past, just be still.

"Be still, and know that I am God! I will be honored by every nation. I will be honored throughout the world." The LORD of Heaven's Armies is here among us; the God of Israel is our fortress. Psalm 46:10-11

At any time that you struggle to remain present in a moment remember these provisions. Write them down and place them in areas where your eyes will always meet them.

1. *Therefore do not be anxious about tomorrow, for tomorrow will be anxious for itself. Sufficient for the day is its own trouble. -Matthew 6:34*

2. *Finally, brothers, whatever is true, whatever is honorable, whatever is just, whatever is pure, whatever is lovely, whatever is commendable, if there is any excellence, if there is anything worthy of praise, think about these things. What you have learned and received and heard and seen in me—practice these things, and the God of peace will be with you. - Phillipians 4: 8-9*

3. *Brothers, I do not consider that I have made it my own. But one thing I do: forgetting what lies behind and straining forward to what lies ahead, I press on toward the goal for the prize of the upward call of God in Christ Jesus.- Phillipians 3:13-14*

Be sure to add your own provisions in the space provided.

XIII. PUSH

In the summer of 2017, my husband and I got pregnant. It was early in our marriage and we knew we had much to accomplish before our baby came. So we planned, waited, and ran rampant in preparation for another human being. At my last doctor's appointment, my nurse told me that my embryo was in the position to miscarry. I didn't believe her and we left. I started speaking over my womb and declaring life.

After visiting the nearest emergency room, I was told that I was still pregnant and nothing seemed wrong. I continued having this sharp pain in my womb and continued telling myself that all would be well and I would pray over my baby's life.

Two days would go by and I revisited the emergency room because I knew something was wrong. I ended up getting a sonogram—no baby. Empty. Destroyed. Forgotten about. Abandoned. Disappointed. It's like nothing ever happened.

So, what's a miscarriage story doing in the middle of a book about faith and entrepreneurship? Tested faith **sharpens** us especially in doubtful situations. One can easily go through a traumatic experience and abandon all faith.

Let me explain: In no world would I think that experiencing this level of pain and heartbreak was necessary. In the most opportune time to doubt God, ironically became the most opportune moment to praise God. This is why: his will never changed for my life.

Some of you have been pregnant with God's vision for you and when it didn't happen in your timing, you began to question God. In that moment, you were experiencing a miscarriage instead of celebrating a birth. The vision fell before it got a chance to fully develop. The opportunity wavered and you felt like someone was playing a sick joke on you.

The enemy began planting seeds of doubt in your mind and told you that you'd never get a chance to experience it again. You felt forgotten about. You felt like you were sitting in darkness and began to ask God "Why me?"

It's in these moments, God is saying "Trust me." It's not an ideal situation, but it still doesn't mean you don't have a **due date**.

There have already been moments in your life that you felt like you were falling apart. You felt like you couldn't push forward using your own fuel. You wanted to give up, but God said PUSH.

The enemy will use moments of misfortune to get you to speak curses over your future. Our words carry so much power. He will take the disappointment of a failed business to make you feel like you'll ever be able to start up another one. He'll make you look at your history of failed relationships and convince you that you'll always be alone. It's in the breaking of old things that new things are birthed.

I didn't know what to do as I was laboring in my bathroom, but I began speaking life. I won't lie to you, I struggled believing it, but I felt like I had to do it. I began declaring my child's name and stating the things that they would do for the Lord.

Somehow, in the strangest and most uncomfortable way, I knew it had to happen this way. I knew it would do nothing but grow me. Heartbreak has a way of bringing us into involuntary submission and it's the perfect pruning ground.

I'd have no way of knowing where you are in your walk. I don't know if you're experiencing the highest height of your life or the darkest, most frightening valley. All I know to tell you is to PUSH. There's something that's birthed in us when we push past what's in front of us and see what's on the other side. It's unusual, uncertain, and nowhere near our natural instinct, but I'm here to tell you that *something* is on the other side of it.

You haven't been left here alone. You may feel like you don't even have the energy to push. Perfect. His strength is made *perfect* in our weakness. With the bit of strength you may have left, speak life. In speaking life, you strengthen your faith and begin to break up the darkness around you.

If you're in a waiting season, let patience complete its perfect work so that you may be fully mature and lacking nothing. God knows of your expectations and desires. He knows the level of faith you'll need to sustain them as well. Nothing is by mistake.

While it may look like other people are planting businesses and they're sprouting overnight, trust God in his timing for you. The timing made for others does NOT make your timing late. Never focus so much on what you've yet to get, that you bypass what God is currently doing in your life. You, at this moment, are sitting in the midst of an answered prayer. You have due dates to honor that God has given you. While planning for your miraculous future is great, bask in the supernatural things that God has done for you to get to this point.

I find that God changes our perception of things in every season. As a faith boss, we learn to adjust our sight based on the season he has us in. What may have been an acceptable push in the last season may require sharpened faith in this current season. Think it not strange when you're challenged on every side, enduring heartbreak, disappointment, and trials. As we discussed before, suffering (when you're rooted in God's word) produces perseverance.

I'm unsure if I'll ever just "welcome" challenges as they come, but I know who stands with me through every step. I know that whatever comes my way, my faith will strengthen. I know with every time I feel something break off of me, I'm aligning closer to Christ. I know that in trusting and submitting that you're purposed for the push.

"In this you greatly rejoice, though now for a little while, if need be, you have been grieved by various trials, that the genuineness of your faith, being much more precious than gold that perishes, though it is tested by fire, may be found to praise, honor, and glory at the revelation of Jesus Christ."- 1 Peter 1:6-7

XIV. Choose Greater

Every day we're faced with decisions that can change the trajectory of our businesses, goals, and lives. Choose greater. So much easier said than done. We often make plans and set expectations that get diluted in life's unexpected twists in turns. Here's one truth: the view from the hill is just as important as the view from the valley. The choice from the valley is just as important as choices made from the hill. It's in hot, uncomfortable, unexpected situations that our habits surface and expose our character.

This chapter will serve as a gentle reminder to choose greater even in the midst of trial. What does this have to do with business? Everything. It has everything to do with our business, marriages, friendships, jobs, self worth, family, and more. We make many good decisions, but hardly enough God decisions.

This book, for instance, was 1000% a God decision and his mercy prevailed as he gave me so much time to write it. Choosing greater is simple, but not easy. Most decisions needing to be made are simple and require a simple yes or no. However, it's our will that must align with our decision.

"Do not, therefore, fling away your [fearless] confidence, for it has a glorious and great reward. For you have need of patient endurance [to bear up under difficult circumstances without compromising], so that when you have carried out the will of God, you may receive and enjoy to the full what is promised."
HEBREWS 10:35-36 AMP

The enemy basks in creating the illusion that you have no choices and likes to default us to fear. Many would argue that fear is natural and if we're put in a situation that calls for our survival skills, fear would be a behavior that helps us identify threats. So this raises the question, is fear a choice?

Is fear something that we can actually help or will we always have at least one fear in this world? One thing that I can recall is that anytime I had a fear as a kid, I had to confront it with what I *knew*. For instance, when I was afraid of the dark, I would confront my dark bedroom by saying out loud that nothing in the room could hurt me. How did I know this? Because the only thing that changed in the room was the absence of light.

If I started empowering the darkness in my childhood bedroom by saying things like "the dark is scary" and "something's going to hurt me", I would have never turned the lights off. If I never chose to give the same hope to the darkness that I gave to the light, I wouldn't have ever had a peaceful night's rest.

Some of y'all are gonna get that one on the way home.

In whatever season you're currently in, choose greater. Not because I told you to, but because it will free you from the bondage of doubt that tells you that you're limited and incapable. Choose greater for your business, family, health, and God given assignments. We choose greater when we TELL those problems and fears exactly what we know!

God is not calling us to be afraid of the world, but overcome it in faith. We have to start speaking to the things that have taken up mental real estate in our minds for so long and remind them that they don't belong there. We have to stand boldly and remind ourselves as well as other believers that peace is indeed our portion. Again, you don't have to go at it in your own strength. Choosing greater is not dependent upon your own wit and intellect, it's dependent on your faith.

Peace I leave with you; my peace I give you. I do not give to you as the world gives. Do not let your hearts be troubled and do not be afraid. -John 14:27

XV. The Power of Unity

Raise your hand if you've ever made the statement: If you want something done right, you've got to do it yourself. Now raise your hand if you've ever tried to embark on a business mission or even complete a small task and realized that you shouldn't have gone at it alone.

Friend, put your hands down.

The world tells us all the time about solo missions and disregards the essence of team. The pride of telling ourselves that we're the star player and that no one else can do what we do is absolute deception. Simply put: we need people. As much as we want to be needed, we have to be honest in evaluating our strengths and weaknesses.

In building your business and obediently working in the assignment that God has called you to, collaboration is unavoidable. I was once the student who hated group projects in school. It never felt fair and always seemed that one group member cared while another group member saw the opportunity for someone else to carry the weight. In experiences such as these, I became frustrated with working with others. I believed that if I worked on my own, my failing was my fault and my winning was my doing.

That, however, is nowhere close to how God sees us as the body of Christ. No one can do everything. In fact, the mindset to even attempt to do everything is disobedient. Let's challenge it: who ACTUALLY said that your way was best?

Pride will have us out here counting out people that we actually need. It will have us measuring our strengths to someone else's weaknesses. It will have us neglecting the fact that our iron needs to be sharpened. We don't only sharpen others. It will ultimately make us a one person show that others don't even want to work with.

In the world of business, connections are of high value. It's how we build collaborations, partnerships, sponsorships, and things of the like. If we're wanting to learn something new, we're supposed to get in a room where there are others who can teach us something. This process is called **networking**. Oftentimes uncomfortable, but necessary to grow your business.

To cast a **net** and essentially make it **work** has been one of the simplest yet complicated measures to date. I've never been fishing before, but the patience that it takes to catch fish is something to be noted. Our network isn't built overnight. It builds when we understand that unity is something that God favors. The body of Christ is a unified body that functions in perfection. It's meant to look like him, not like us.

"Again, the kingdom of heaven is like a net that was thrown into the sea and gathered fish of every kind. -Matthew 13:47

Unifying your team, family, or ministry requires obedience and mending of the net. Our "nets" are usually torn from unbelief, disappointment, doubt, fear, and any other concoction that the enemy can cook up. We are called to be fishers of men and our nets are useless if we never repair them.

For so long, conflicts have been labeled as the "finisher of relationships". We allow the friction that occurs between personalities and misread communication be the deciding factor in our usefulness for others. We walk away from people and things that don't meet us where we are. We lack understanding and reasoning because we refuse to abandon our opinions. Thus, here we are with a divided vision all because of conflict.

Seasoned business owners will admit that conflict can be used as a form of team-building when facilitated from a place of resolution. If we begin to look at conflict as an opportunity for growth instead of defeat, we can unify and be unbreakable.

Much of my struggle in trusting God and developing my faith is that I wrongly saw God the way I saw people. I transferred much of my disappointing experience to my walk with Christ and struggled. God is not people. People are not God. We can't hold an everlasting God to the standard of imperfect people who are changing every day. Could you imagine if God treated us the way we treat each other?

As we discussed in the "Obedience" chapter, you won't always understand what God is telling you to do, but this doesn't mean that you disobey. Specifically with God's people, we should always concern ourselves with our nets. Is our net perfect to our standards, yet not catching any fish? Are we refusing to patch up the holes?

Fishermen regularly maintain their nets. They don't save the opportunity to repair it for a certain fish. They maintain their nets for all fish. It's in the maintenance of securing our nets that makes our nets less likely to break. The disciples were actually asked to go deeper into the water, past their comfort zone, to launch their nets.

And when he had finished speaking, he said to Simon, "Put out into the deep and let down your nets for a catch." And Simon answered, "Master, we toiled all night and took nothing! But at your word I will let down the nets." And when they had done this, they enclosed a large number of fish, and their nets were breaking.- Luke 5:4-6

Jesus didn't even go at it alone. While he walked this earth in a human shell, he was still the all knowing, all powerful son of God. Jesus MASTERED the art of team. There is no "I" in team, but there is definitely one in FAILURE. If you're being called to lead, check your net. It matters not the size of your following. The fish that you have, whether few or many, need to be secured in a net. They need to see the surrendering to God in you.

In the proper steps of forgiveness, repentance, and resolution, all begin with a surrenderance. Without surrenderance, it's nearly impossible to properly resolve and unify. Everybody doesn't need to be right. Everyone needs to know how to work together. Everyone doesn't need to be the boss or the leader. A FaithBoss pursues all things with the salvation of others in mind.

In our interaction with people, we must learn to be sensitive to the fact that we may be the ONLY introduction to Christ that someone may have received up until this point. This is not an urge to play "perfect Christian", but to lead from a place of honesty and share the transformation that God has done in you.

If someone is ever questioning the efficiency of their team, I'd ask them immediately about their unity. This isn't to be confused with how well they get along and how nice they are to one another, but how they *complement* one another in their strengths and weaknesses. I'd ask about how conflicts are handled and how *quickly* they're handled. I'd ask if each team member is held accountable to a provision. Does the supervisor know the goals and intentions of each team member? Do they know how to nurture it? I'd ask if everyone within the team had a full understanding of their role and function and if they understood the order of the company. Companies don't need massage chairs in the employee's lounge as much as they need to understand the relevance of unity.

XVI. Take Flight!

All things that go up must come down. Planes, meteors, insects with wings, etc. All have a starting point and then they soar. It's easy to become obsessed with just taking flight. Just pressing "publish" or launching a new venture are enough to make most 'high' (pun intended) from the feelings of instant success. While it takes a lot to just take flight, very few are prepared for what happens while in the air.

It's take off time. Our business plan is solidified, business cards are printed, social media pages have been created, we've obtained the necessary licenses and certification to run our businesses. We're running with our idea at full speed and feel the wind beneath our wings at takeoff.

It's important to get systems in order when you're getting ready to take off as certain unchecked bags can affect your acceleration. When weighed down with fear, you will not continue to soar. If you lead with turbulence, you will be in for an early landing. If you try to pilot, you may very well end up hurting not only yourself, but your *passengers*.

Business owners who have been in the game for a while will be the first to tell you that launching is a balancing act. Getting a business off of the ground in its entirety is it's own feat, but maintaining it while it's in the air comes with it's own set of rules. There's maintenance that comes with maintaining the height that you've accelerated, but what does it take to go higher? Another question that one would ask is "what does it take not to crash?"

If launching guarantees you anything, it guarantees unpredictabilities. Our positioning before taking off is extremely important. At this moment, our foundation matters more than anything. Turbulence can be anything from shaky finances to an unexpected event turning your business upside down. The goal in launching is not try to *control* the turbulence, but to press past the opposition with strategy.

"Everyone then who hears these words of mine and does them will be like a wise man who built his house on the rock. And the rain fell, and the floods came, and the winds blew and beat on that house, but it did not fall, because it had been founded on the rock. And everyone who hears these words of mine and does not do them will be like a foolish man who built his house on the sand. And the rain fell, and the floods came, and the winds blew and beat against that house, and it fell, and great was the fall of it."-Matthew 7:24-27

After most of us get a great idea, we want the fastest and most promising route of getting to success. In that moment, many will consult any and everyone but God about their vision. We begin to put our trust in others who may claim to hold the secrets to success, but are trying to sell us back our own dream. This can easily end up being one of those unchecked bags that we discussed earlier.

The launch matters, but the landing is what makes the launch count. Are we familiar with how to counteract the wind speeds when crossing into different territory? Will we remain focused when the clouds are blocking the view we have? As Faith Bosses, we have to only be willing to build what's worthy of withstanding unexpected impact.

When our foundation is shaky, all that we build upon it will be unstable. When we take off after a launch, we need to be able to withstand the turbulence without going into a tailspin. From the launch, we should never separate our faith from our works. We must remember that we're carrying cargo, but every bag must be checked for it's contents. Our passengers need to land safely and when we get to our destination, we have another journey ahead of us. The flight ahead is much bigger than you, proceed with faith not caution.

XVII. Advance Past Winning

After launching that GOD idea, it's natural to receive positive feedback. Many will be shocked that you stepped out and did something new, some may have seen it coming, but not nearly as soon, and some may even have a hard time with your new venture.

The truth is this: when embarking on your God given task in uncharted territory, you are indeed shattering the glass ceiling. God may be calling you to break barriers in your family. Maybe no one else has done it, but that doesn't mean it's impossible. Shattering the glass ceiling means breaking through barriers, possibly getting cut, and creating a path for the next person. You feel the impact first and there may even be a little bit of blood. Now imagine if God has a highrise for you in mind. Yikes.

The feeling of "winning" doesn't always come with a prize. It may actually come with a lot of questions and opposition. It actually may come with a lot of breaking and rebuilding. The world will tell us that every new level will require more of us, but it actually doesn't. It requires less of us and more of him.

In your obedience, you may even spark a catalytic movement. You're winning and you know it, but have you made it clear that God still deserves all of the praise? Are people seeing you or him?

If you find yourself in the pioneering position, don't merely identify yourself with winning alone. While God has made you more than a conqueror, he's ironically put us in a winning position to lose.

Let me explain.

We must learn to advance past winning alone. Our winning is not solely for us. It's not for our name to be on display. In fact, our winning is in vain it doesn't point people back to Christ. Our "losing" is to be in the areas of vanity, slack, pride, and arrogance.

While "lifting as we climb" has become a popular mantra in the planning and development stages of your journey, how do we confront those feelings that tell us we "earned" all that we're getting? The 'self made' attitude that reminds us that no one else was with us shooting in the gym and that we deserve to win.

I'd love to preach a ho-hum message of prosperity and gifts and while all that God has in store for you is entirely in store for YOU, he's not a God that stops growing you when you reach a pinnacle point. Challenges are not an exemption once you reach a certain level of influence. He cares about your legacy, generations to come, those attached to you, and how his name is glorified through your obedience.

God's blessings do not begin or end with profit. Anyone can profit. God sustains and takes our reach to new realms. In the losing of ourselves, we gain more of him. God wants us to advance past winning and our comfortability zone.

For I know the plans I have for you, declares the Lord, plans for welfare and not for evil, to give you a future and a hope. Then you will call upon me and come and pray to me, and I will hear you. You will seek me and find me, when you seek me with all your heart. I will be found by you, declares the Lord, and I will restore your fortunes and gather you from all the nations and all the places where I have driven you, declares the Lord, and I will bring you back to the place from which I sent you into exile. - Jeremiah 29:11-14

Our treasures in heaven trump our treasures on earth. Faith Bosses aren't in it for the instant gratification, but the long haul. Advancing past winning means to get over ourselves and trust God's direction for us. Our riches and successes can't save our soul. Our self-glorification can't bring someone out of darkness.

God doesn't stop transforming us even in unfortunate circumstances he's looking for fruit. He is the true vine and our fruit is directly grown from our connection to him. It's in advancing beyond the idea of being the best or having the most that we can see beyond ourselves.

Our winning is actually not about us. As great as it feels to be on top and to have conquered something, it's all in vain if our heart isn't grounded in encouraging those around us. As you're building, launching, or refining, check your heart. We all want to win, it's our human instinct. In this case, we win by losing and gain by giving.

FaithBoss Plans of Action

"Let the [spoken] word of Christ have its home within you [dwelling in your heart and mind—permeating every aspect of your being] as you teach [spiritual things] and admonish and train one another with all wisdom, singing psalms and hymns and spiritual songs with thankfulness in your hearts to God. Whatever you do [no matter what it is] in word or deed, do everything in the name of the Lord Jesus [and in dependence on Him], giving thanks to God the Father through Him."

COLOSSIANS 3:16-17 AMP

Within this book, I've shared different revelations that God has downloaded me with over time as he's shaped me into a Faith Boss. Over time, a frustration of mine has been that building businesses has been regarded as secret when there are tools that can help business owners within the word of God.

In the development of HustleBlendz™ , a coffee company that my husband Tweety and I built, we found that the world's idea of owning and operating a business pales in comparison to what God wants us to do as Faith Bosses. We're a faith-based coffee company that roasts fresh coffee beans and pride ourselves on being ethical and delivering exceptional customer service. Every day we're learning and growing our business with God as the CEO.

The following pages will serve as guidelines to aid you in organizing your ideas, strategies, and hopefully help you answer some questions regarding your God given business idea. If you already own a business, use these tools to help you flesh out new ideas or seek new revelation regarding your existing business.

We make many plans along the way. We know that success isn't a straight path, but somehow, we even think that our multiple plans that we devise even after Plan A are bulletproof as well. In this section of the book, instead of making *your* plans known to God, you will make God's plans known to *you*. No more dead works and empty deeds. No more hustling and doing just enough to make ends meet. You've been called to lead a kingdom business. Within the next few pages are *practical* and *applicable* tools that will help you form or even fine tune your business.

Proverbs 16:3-4 says *"Commit your works to the Lord [submit and trust them to Him] and your plans will succeed [if you respond to His will and guidance].*

In the following table, write down, in detail, what God has told you to do so far. This is not something that anyone else will see unless you show it to them.

What *exactly* has God told you to do?	**When** did he tell you to do it?	**What** have you started so far?	**How** will you know it's complete?

Faith Boss Business Core Values

You've already written the vision and made it plain. Now it's time to specify what your assignment stands for. In detail, you'll complete the table and write the overview of your business and what your business can do for others.

Objective	
• Write an <u>overview</u> of your business in at least 1-2 sentences. What do people _need_ to know about your business?	
• What problem does your business solve? Describe your product or services. Refer to them as solutions.	

Mission Statement	
• What are you on a mission to achieve? How can your consumers or target audience be a part of that? • What are the core values of your business? While many other things in business will change, what are the values that will never change?	
Branding	
• How will you brand your product or service to stand out from others? What makes your brand distinct and memorable? • What colors, words, and emotions are associated with your brand?	

Vision and Goals

- See.E.O, what foresight are you casting for the business? Where do you see it going in 1 month? 6 months? 1 year?

- Specify any goals that you have. Be detailed about what those goals will look like and give them *due dates* to hold yourself accountable.

- Short term measurable goals?

- Long term measurable goals?

Faith Boss SWOP Analysis

In this section, you will complete a **SWOP** Analysis to identify your company's weaknesses and provisions, as well as its strengths and the potential opportunities you plan to develop.

Strengths What are some strengths and advantages that you've observed in your business? In your FaithBoss leadership?	
Weaknesses What areas have an opportunity for growth? Where are you at a disadvantage? Where could you use assistance?	

Opportunities

What opportunities are currently in your reach? How could you make the best of them? How can you turn one of your strengths into a viable opportunity?

Provisions

What biblically sound provision can be put in place regarding your analysis of your business? What scriptures are keeping you accountable and focused

Faith Boss Financial Plan

• List all materials and services you will need to start. Research and calculate ALL costs associated with your startup • What are your *recurring* expenses? Is there a way to lower or eliminate a percentage of this number?	
• How have you budgeted on startup costs? Will you need extra funds? Will you be taking out a loan? Applying for a grant to supplement your costs? Looking for an investor? List and evaluate the sources of your startup costs	
How are you positioning yourself for profit? How are you pricing your	

goods or services? What are you projections looking like for the next month, quarter, or year?	
How are you paying yourself while building your business? If any, how are you managing your personal debt while building your business wealth? What's your business savings strategy? How are you giving?	
Specify the following. **Envision** where you want to see yourself and give yourself a realistic date to get there. (MAKE IT PLAIN) • Annual gross income made by company • Your salary • List the roles needed for your company. Specify what each position will be paid. • Estimate your monthly expenses • Write, in detail, how you will steward the increase.	

FaithBoss Marketing Plan

This section should detail who your target customers are, how you plan on reaching them, what channels you'll use to reach them, and how you'll position your business to your audience.

<u>**Who are your consumers?**</u>
One of the biggest mistakes that one can make is believing that everyone is their customer. In this section, you'll create a profile of your ideal client.
 	
     • Age Range
 	
     • Gender
 	
     • Location
 	
     • Income
 	
     • Occupation	

Who is your target buyer person?

If your vision is to expand your brand to different buyers and retail outlets eventually, what kind of buyer are you trying to appeal to?

Production

- How much does it take to create your product?

- If you're service based, how much time does it cost you to deliver your service?

- What are your production methods? Will you be needing to use another company to complete your production?

- How much will it cost you to sell your product?

Quality Check

- Describe the experience that you want your customers to walk away with.

- How will you maintain consistency in your product or service?

- How will your product be different from others?

Accessibility

- Where will your customers find you?

- Do you have a physical location? If you're planning on getting one, be descriptive in how you'd like it to look.

- If you're mainly an e-commerce business, are you present and consistent on all social media outlets? Can anyone find you easily understand your objective?

Customer Relationship Management

- What are the touchpoints that you will use to stay connected to your customers? Birthdays?

| Customer rewards points? Discounts?

 • What are your customer service policies?

 • How will you increase customer retention and secure long term clients?

 • How will customers be communicated with and at what frequency? | |

Faith Boss Plan of Order

This section will detail the legal environment that your business will thrive in. As Faith Bosses, we want no *unchecked bags* to weigh down our flight. As you are developing a business or fine tuning an existing business, it's imperative to make sure that we've done our homework on what it takes to keep us in flight.

| Does your business need any licenses or permits? | |

Have you obtained or in the process of obtaining any trademarks, copyrights, or patents? FaithBosses <u>own their smarts.</u>	
Does your business require insurance coverage? How much of an expense will it be?	
Do you have an understanding of contracts and invoices? Will you be needing either for your transactions?	
Based on the structure of your business, Is it a sole proprietorship, partnership, corporation, or limited liability corporation?	

Short Term Goal: **(feel free to complete for all short term goals)** **Anticipated** **Deadline**_____	

Action Step 1: • What will you do first? • What will be your first practical step? • How will you know it's complete? • When will it be done?	
Action Step 2: • Building off of your first step, what can be done next? • *Make it simple, but make it effective.* • How will you know it's complete? • When will it be done?	
Action Step 3: • Assess your first two steps, what has been the outcome? • What opportunities are you currently present for you based off of your first steps? • What's the best practical step now? • How will you know it's complete? • When will it be done?	
Continue with detailed, well-thought out action steps until you've accomplished your short term goal.	

Long Term Goal: **(feel free to complete for all long term goals)** **Anticipated** **Deadline:_____**	

Action Step 1: • What will you do first? • What will be your first practical step? • How will you know it's complete? • When will it be done?	
Action Step 2: • Building off of your first step, what can be done next? • *Make it simple, but make it effective.* • How will you know it's complete? • When will it be done?	
Action Step 3: • Assess your first two steps, what has been the outcome? • What opportunities are you currently present for you based off of your first steps? • What's the best practical step now? • How will you know it's complete? • When will it be done?	
Continue with detailed, well-thought out action steps until you've accomplished your long term goal.	

Reflection: Now that you've broken up your goal(s) into action steps, how do you feel? What provisions did you include into your action steps? What was the final outcome? Did anything take a different direction? Write about it.

_____

_____

_____

_____

_____

_____

_____

_____

_____

Consider this a starting point for fleshing out specifics for your business. This is something that can be completed over time as you continue to ask God for specifics concerning your business. The Faith Boss plans are meant to structure and organize our thoughts and ideas. They should be made visible when you're planning and visualizing your business.

Glossary

(Because I like to make up a lot of terms)

1. **#FaithBoss** (n)- (1) an individual who has dedicated their works to Christ and operates with him being the source. (2) This individual is obedient to the missions that God has laid before them and wastes no time to fulfill duties at the appointed time. (3) Individual serves as the creative operator in the business/assignment that God has called them to.

2. **Relentless Faith** (n)- An attitude that makes faith the only option. When one is deemed as *relentless,* they're stubbornly zeroed in on what's in front of them with no excuses.

3. **Brokivation**-(noun) (1) The state of being motivated by shortage of resources. (2) The ability to create, innovate, repurpose, and initiate something with no excuses of financial standing. (3) the act of purposefully creating abundance without an abundance of resources.

4. **See.E.O**- (noun) (1) One who trusts the vision of God to lead them in their endeavors without much worldly confirmation. Also known as one who **Sets Executive Order** and hears from God to order their steps. A FaithBoss is a See.E.O who knows that God spearheads their business.

5. **Thoughtful Interruptions**- using provisions from the Bible to keep your mind aligned.

6. **Unbothered**- A place of peace and full trust in God that doesn't let you get tripped up by the little things. Not to be confused with being nonchalant or dismissive. Being unbothered means choosing what and when we respond to things.

7. **Response-ability**- a reminder that we have choices in the way that we respond to things around us. Everything doesn't deserve an emotional response or a response from a place of uncertainty. Give things your best response.

Dedication to my FaithBoss Community

I had to write the book that I needed to read. I had us in mind. We need more influencers, innovators, creatives, entrepreneurs, leaders, and more standing up for the very first creator. As my husband, Tweety Angwenyi, says, "Pursuit is what separates doers and thinkers. More of us need to pursue Christ with our entire life."

Today, pursue Christ first. Being a faith boss is defined as one who is living by faith, walking by faith, *building* by faith, *creating* by faith, and *operating* by faith. Oftentimes, faith is written off as "blind trust", but the book of Hebrews will remind us that 'it's the substance of things hoped for and evidence of things not seen'. It's far more than just a belief or feeling, it's a lifestyle. It's the trust and confident peace that you were created with purpose and promise.

Let's stop writing and erasing and set our intentions on what we've been called to. We can't however, just run with the vision with no plan. What sense would that make? Consider this a call to action, a challenge, a measure of accountability. We've discuss being a See.E.O vs. CEO, due vs. do season, the power of vision, and much more that will assist with your #FaithBoss journey.

You're made for this. It's time. It's time to take your business plan to God. It's time to rid ourselves of excuses and walk in complete authority. It's about more than just an idea or the possibility of making money.

You didn't stumble upon this book by mistake. In and by faith, the vision that God has set aside just for you has been left in your hands to carry out. Join our Faith Boss community at www.faithboss.org and inform us of all of the GOD things you're doing!

A Prayer For The Faith Boss

Gracious Father, I thank you for the hands that are holding this book. I thank you for the life and purpose that you've planted inside of them. Remind them that what you began you will sustain and complete in them. When the days are hard and they feel like giving up, remind them that they're not alone or forgotten about. May they seek you as they embark on a journey to diligently complete what you've put in front of them.

May you keep their eyes focused on you and eliminate distractions. Remind them of their truth and that you have a plan for them. In whatever season they're in, peace is their portion.

Lord, I thank you for the life of the Faith Boss reading this. I thank you for their family and loved ones. Lord, may you supply every need. Let there be no area of lack. Let there be no division from the assignment that you have for them. May they have a heart of forgiveness, love, and obedience.

Lord, you have called them out in this moment for a reason. Even if we don't understand what you're doing in our lives, we thank you anyway. We thank you for every time you've covered us and breathed breath into our bodies. I declare it now that this Faith Boss will do great things in your name.

In Jesus name, Amen.

Made in the USA
Monee, IL
08 June 2020

32841135R00074